CHURCH
MEMBERSHIP

CHURCH MEMBERSHIP

FOUNDATIONAL PRINCIPLES

KEVIN J. CONNER

Published by Conner Ministries Ltd
WEB: kevinconner.org
Email: kevin.conner321@gmail.com

Visit www.amazon.com/author/kevinjconner for a list of other books by Kevin Conner.

CONNER
MINISTRIES

FOUNDATIONAL PRINCIPLES OF CHURCH MEMBERSHIP

TABLE OF CONTENTS

PREFACE

It was in 1972 that we, as the Conner family, moved to Portland, Oregon, USA. Instead of living there for one year, it turned out to be ten years in the will of God. Our time as a family was at Bible Temple (now City Bible), with Dick (K.R.) Iverson, the then-senior minister of Bible Temple. These were wonderful years, as God built the Church under Dick's leadership along with a wonderful team of elders and leaders.

It was in these early years that the whole matter of "**Church Membership**" came up. They were days – even as it is for many now – when people did not seem to have any desire for being a committed member of any Church. Many reasons were given Lack of commitment in marriage, lack of commitment in the home, in the work place, as well as lack of commitment in Church life characterized the times. People just did not want to be committed members to anything, to anyone or anywhere. They just wanted to be 'free' to do whatever they believed the Lord wanted them to do; come, stay or go, as they liked. The truth of the matter is, nothing can be built with any stability without commitment. Marriage, homes, work, Churches – nothing can have a lasting effect if there is no commitment.

This Course (originally, **"Principles of Church Life"**) actually arose out of the need to see people, who wanted to, become **voluntary committed members** in the local Church where the Lord was planting them.

These Lessons (condensed to 12 Lessons here), became a must for all who desired to be members in Bible Temple. Once the Lessons were completed, all had the opportunity to make application for membership and come into commitment. This commitment was a mutual commitment between the eldership and members as all were committed to the Lord.

Over the years, one of the great strengths of the Church (Bible Temple) was the voluntary committed membership. It must be emphasized that it was **voluntary**. One cannot legislate love, loyalty or commitment. People should not be forced or coerced into Church membership. They should not do it because they 'have to' but because they 'love to' and because they believe this is God's will for them in that local Church.

In 1981 we returned as a family (except our daughter, Sharon and son-in-law, Frank Damazio), and became part of Waverley Christian Fellowship, with Richard J.Holland. A similar situation was evident at that time regarding membership. After much prayer, the decision was made to introduce **"Principles of Church Life"** for those who desired to become voluntary committed members. God placed His seal on it as we obeyed the Lord on the matter.

Questions most frequently asked were: "What does Waverley Christian Fellowship believe? How does one become identified with this local Church? How can a person become a voluntary committed member?" For this reason, this basic, elementary introductory Catechism was designed. Upon full attendance and/or completion of all the Lessons, people were free to make application for membership. Those received into membership were received by the "right hands of fellowship" (Gal.2:9), and received a Membership Certificate.

Most denominations have some form of instruction (or Catechism) that people complete before becoming committed members of the Church. So Waverley follows the same procedures for membership.

Since that original 'Membership Commitment Sunday', one of the great strengths of Waverley Christian Fellowship is that of committed members. This Course has continued over many years and is a must for all who want to make Waverley their 'home Church'. All those who want to be involved in any area of leadership take this Course and become committed members. Everybody is welcome to attend the Fellowship but commitment becomes the strength of any local Church. In the Book of Acts "they **continued stedfastly** in the apostles doctrine, and in fellowship and in the breaking of bread and in prayers" (Acts 2:42). They were committed to the Lord and to the local Church where God had planted them.

Because we are living in an age of great deception, and many religious cults and philosophies abound, it is important that the sincere seeker after truth prove that which is of "the spirit of truth" and "the spirit of error." This can only be done by an appeal to the only infallible revelation God has given to mankind, and that is, the Word of God, the Holy Bible. The Scriptures alone are the final authority for all matters of faith and practice.

While it is to be recognized that no one can confine God to mere "articles of faith", it is also to be recognized that **sound, wholesome, healthy doctrine** is important in these days. Believers are not to be "tossed (like ships) to and fro between chance gusts of teaching, and wavering with every changing wind of doctrine, (the prey of) the cunning craftiness and cleverness of unscrupulous men, (gamblers engage) in every shifting form of trickery in inventing error to be misled" (Ephes.4:14. Amplified New Testament).

Over the years, a number of ministers have asked about this Membership Course, whether it was possible to use them in their own Fellowships for those desirous of becoming members. Because of this these Lessons are set out here in a more permanent form under the title **"Foundational Principles of Church Membership."** They are sent forth to be a blessing to those who want to establish voluntary committed membership in their local Church.

The format is similar to a Catechism. "Catechism" simply defined means: "Instruction by asking questions, providing and correcting the answers." It is one of the oldest methods of teaching and is still one of the best. Whether Teacher/Instructor or Student/Member, as the Lessons are worked through and the Scriptures read, the answers for the "fill-in's" can be found at the back of the text.

Every person who desires to become a committed member of a New Testament local Church should have these principles laid as a sure foundation in their lives. They should not just know these things theoretically but should know them experientially. Committed members are those who have **experienced the truth** of these Lessons It is experiencing truth, not only knowing the truth, that counts!

Most of these Lessons have been adapted from the original textbooks by Kevin J.Conner and K.R."Dick" Iverson (ISBN 0-914936-23-9, 1976. Copyright, Bible Temple Publications). Some sections have been updated and rewritten to make them more adaptable for other leaders and ministers in the Body of Christ and their local situation.

They are sent forth, not to be used in a letteristic manner but creatively, to lay a good foundation in the lives of all who desire to become voluntary committed members in a New Testament local Church. The key is found in John 6:63. Jesus said, "The **words** I speak, they are **spirit** and they are **life**." It is the Spirit who gives life to the words. If there is no spirit, there is no life, just words!

Kevin J.Conner

January, 2001

FOREWORD

Relative to the matter of "Church Membership", the question arises: "Where can we go to find anything pertaining to this?" The answer: "Go to the Bible; go to the book of beginnings of Church life; go to the Book of Acts!" In the Gospels, Jesus said that He would build the Church (Matthew 16:15-19). In the Book of Acts, Jesus is building His Church by the power of the Holy Spirit (Acts 2:47 A.V.)

Over many years of study in the Word of God, especially on that which concerns the Church, one needs to go back to the Book of Acts to see what it was like "in the beginning".

Acts chapter 2 is undoubtedly the most important chapter in the Book of Acts, as all the subsequent chapters and events are built on the things that took place in this chapter. A consideration of Acts 2 provides us with five "originals" and these become the foundations upon which these Principles for Church Membership are built. These "originals" are:

1. **The Original Church**
   Here the promise and prophecy of Jesus concerning the building of His Church begins to be fulfilled. The original Church began in Jerusalem.

2. **The Original Pentecost**
   Here in Jerusalem was the original Pentecostal outpouring of the Holy Spirit. It was the first or initial Pentecost. It was the birthday of the New Testament Church. It was indeed a "healthy birth". This outpouring of the Spirit was the beginning of the fulfilment of Joel's prophecy concerning the last days (Joel 2:28-32).

3. **The Original Sermon**
   Here we have Peter's first sermon, as he is filled with the Holy Spirit. It was the foundational sermon, the dedicatory message for the Church. All other sermons in Acts are based on the content of Peter's Pentecostal message in Acts 2.

4. **The Original Kingdom Keys**
   Here we see the apostle Peter using the "keys of the kingdom" as promised to him by the Lord Jesus Christ. Jesus said that He would build His Church and He would give to Peter the "keys of the kingdom". In Acts, Peter uses these keys to open the door of faith to both Jews (Acts 2) and Gentiles (Acts 10-11).

5. **The Original Church Members**
   Here in Acts 2, in response to Peter's word and the convicting power of the Holy Spirit, 3000 people were "added to the Church" (Acts 2:42-47 A.V.). These were the original members, the first members added to the 120 disciples in the upper room. They continued steadfastly in the apostles doctrine and fellowship (Acts 2:42).

If we could ask the original members of the original Church how they were "added to the Church", and what were the pre-requisites to membership, what would they tell us? Well, this is what **"Foundational Principles of Church Membership"** is all about. We are going back to the beginning, back to the original Church at Jerusalem. Here we discover principles for belonging to His Church that have never changed. Over Church history, people have deviated from "the original" but God's plan, purpose, and will have never changed.

Welcome to "**Foundational Principles of Church Membership**". The Teacher/Instructor and Student/Member is encouraged to read the Scripture references along with the Lesson and complete the "fill-ins" (answers at the back of the book), as they lay "a good foundation" for Christian living and committed Church membership.

LESSON ONE

THE NEW TESTAMENT CHURCH

"the Lord added to the church daily those who were being saved." (Acts 2:47)

The Bible teaches that it is important for all those who are truly saved to be added to a New Testament local church and have a home church in which they can grow spiritually, be cared for properly and use their gifts to help others.

This instantly raises questions such as, "What exactly is a New Testament Church?" and "How were those early converts *added to the church*?" The Bible provides us with the answers, some of which are addressed in this study.

A. WHAT IS THE CHURCH?

1. The Church is not:

(a) _____

(b) _____

(c) _____

2. The Church is:

(a) _____ Matthew 16:18

(b) _____ Hebrews 10:25

(c) _____ Ephesians 2:19-22

(d) _____ 1 Corinthians 12:12-14

B. WHAT DID JESUS SAY ABOUT THE CHURCH?
Read Matthew 16:18-19; 18:15-20

1. It would be a Church He would build.

2. It would be a Church against which the Gates of Hell would not prevail.

3. It would be a Church that would have the Keys of the Kingdom.

4. It would be a Church that would have a binding ministry.

5. It would be a Church that would have a loosing ministry.

6. It would be a Church that would have a disciplinary ministry.

7. It would be a Church that Christ as risen Head would be "in the midst".

C. WHAT ARE THE TWO BASIC CONCEPTS OF THE NEW TESTAMENT CHURCH ?

1. <u>In the Gospels</u> :
   - ❖ The Church Universal   Matthew 16:15-19.
   - ❖ The Church Local   Matthew 18:15-20.

2. <u>In the Acts and Epistles</u> :
   - ❖ The Church Universal   Ephesians 1:21-23.
          Ephesians 5:25-27.
          Colossians 1:18.

   - ❖ The Church Local   Acts 9:31
          Romans 16:4,16.
          1 Corinthians 16:1,19.
          2 Corinthians 8:1.

D. HOW WERE THE EARLY CONVERTS ADDED TO THE NEW TESTAMENT CHURCH?

1. They were first _____ Acts 5:12-14; 11:24
2. They were then _____ Acts 2:41,47.

E. WHAT ARE THE BASIC BIBLICAL STEPS INVOLVED IN BECOMING AND REMAINING A NEW TESTAMENT CHURCH MEMBERS?

1. _____ Acts 2:44; 8:47.
2. _____ Acts 2:38.
3. _____ Acts 2:38,41.
4. _____ Acts 2:38-39.
5. _____ Acts 2:42.
6. _____ Acts 2:42.
7. _____ Acts 2:42.
8. _____ Acts 2:42.

F. WHAT IS THE PURPOSE OF THE CHURCH'S EXISTENCE?

1. _____
2. _____
3. _____

LESSON TWO

REPENTANCE FROM DEAD WORKS

A. WHAT IS THE FIRST WORD OF THE GOSPEL?

The first word of the Gospel is—————————————————.

The second word is —————————————————(Mark 1:15).

1. John's first message was repentance. (Matthew 3:1-8).

2. Jesus Christ's first message was repentance. (Matthew 4:17).

3. The twelve apostles preached repentance. (Mark 6:7-13).

4. The first message by Peter on the day of Pentecost was "repent". (Acts 2:38).

5. Paul's first message was repentance. (Acts 20:20-21).

Repentance is the first step in the believer's life; God commands it. If this foundation is not properly laid, the whole structure will be shaky, unable to stand the tests and trials that come. "And the times of this ignorance God winked at; but now commands all men everywhere to repent."

Hebrews speaks of it as the "foundation of repentance from dead works". (Hebrews 6:1-2).

B. WHAT ARE SOME FALSE CONCEPTS CONCERNING REPENTANCE?

1. _____ Genesis 6:3; Acts 24:24-25.
   Conviction precedes repentance, but not all who are convicted repent. John 16:8.

2. _____ 2 Corinthians 7:10.
   Worldly sorrow is simply being sorry "for getting caught", but not being sorry for the crime committed.

3. _____
   Reformation is "turning over a new leaf", but not genuine repentance.

4. _____ Matthew 5:20;3:7-12;23:1-28
   The Pharisees in Christ's day were extremely religious, yet they were hypocrites. They never experienced repentance.

5. _____ James 2:19-20.
   Mental faith is merely a mental acceptance and assent to a set of creeds or doctrines, but without any change in the life. This is dead faith.

C. WHAT ARE "DEAD WORKS"?

Paul speaks of _____ befitting repentance. (Acts 26:20)

Dead works are the religious works of the unsaved (Hebrews 6:1-2; 9:14). They may even be seen as good works done by non-Christians.

Dead works are the works of the flesh that have to be repented of. A person dead in sin can only produce dead works (Galatians 5:19-21; Ephesians 2:1; 1 Timothy 5:6).

Dead works are to be repented of so that we may do **good works** and glorify our Father in heaven (Matthew 5:16; James 2:18).

D. WHAT IS THE PROPER ROOT OF REPENTANCE ?

Matthew 3:8 speaks of the _____ of repentance. The root meaning of the word **repentance** is *a change of mind, or a change of heart and attitude*, and this in particular, concerning sin and relationship with God. It means a complete turn; a change of direction.

The Fall brought about in man a mindset that is in rebellion against God and His Law; a mind which desires to go its own way. Isaiah 53:6 reads *All we like sheep have gone astray; we have turned everyone to his own way; and the Lord has laid on him the iniquity of us all.* (See also Ephesians 2:3; Colossians 1:21). **Repentance, brought about by the Holy Spirit, is a change of mind; a facing towards God**. No person can or will repent by himself (1 Timothy 2:25; Romans 2:4), but true repentance is brought about by the conviction of the Holy Spirit; God grants and demands repentance.

Romans 2:4 reads *Or do you despise the riches of His goodness, forbearance and longsuffering; not knowing that the goodness of God leads you to repentance?* (Compare Acts 5:31).

Ern Baxter defines repentance as:
> Repentance is the informing and changing of the <u>mind</u>; the stirring and directing of the <u>emotions</u> to urge the required change; and the action of the <u>will</u> in turning the whole man away from sin and unto God.

Example: The Prodigal Son (Luke 15:11-14).

GOD

SIN

E. WHAT ARE SOME OF THE FRUITS OF GENUINE REPENTANCE?

The fruits of repentance are evidenced in:

1. _____ 2 Corinthians 7:9-11

2. _____ Psalm 32:1-5; 1 John 1:9

3. _____ Proverbs 28:13

4. _____ Ezekiel 36:31-33

5. _____ Leviticus 6:1-7; Luke 19:8

Without these fruits being evident in one's life, there is no genuine repentance in the Biblical sense! Repentance is not a once only thing. It needs to continue as part of the life of the Christian; as God exposes and convicts of things in our lives that need to be dealt with, we must confess and put these things off.

FAITH TOWARDS GOD

A. FAITH TOWARDS GOD

1. The second word of the Gospel is _____

2. Jesus preached _____ and _____ Mark 1:15.

3. Paul preached _____ and _____ Acts 20:21.

4. The second principle of the doctrine of Christ is _____
   Hebrews 6:1. This is not having "faith in our faith", nor "faith in ourselves".

B. HOW IMPORTANT IS FAITH?

Faith is the foundation of the entire Christian life. *For he who comes to God must believe* _____ (Hebrews 11:6).

John 1:12 says *But as many as received Him, to them He gave the right to become the children of God, to those who* _____
The just shall live by faith (Romans 1:17; Habakkuk 2:4). Nothing can be known or received of God unless man first believes in His existence; and secondly, that God has revealed Himself in His Word, the Bible.

C. WHAT ARE SOME FALSE CONCEPTS ABOUT FAITH?

1. _____

2. _____

3. _____

4. _____

D. WHAT IS FAITH?

Now faith is the assurance [the confirmation, the title deed] of the things [we] hope for, being the proof of things [we] do not see and the conviction of their reality – faith perceiving as real fact what is not revealed to his senses. (Hebrew 11:1 Amp.)

1. Faith (noun) – faith, belief, firm persuasion, assurance, firm conviction, honesty, integrity, faithfulness, truthfulness.

2. Believe (verb) – to trust in; put faith in, confide in, rely on a person, or thing, have a mental persuasion; to entrust, commit to the charge or power of (2 Timothy 1:12).

E. WHAT IS THE SOURCE OF TRUE FAITH?

The only source of true Biblical faith is the Word of God, ——————————————

———————————————————————————— See Romans 10:4-17.

The Word of God comes in a variety of ways:

1. The Word spoken in creation.   Genesis 1; John 1:1-3
2. The prophetic Word.   2 Peter 1:20-21
3. The written Word (Logos).   Luke 24:44
4. The Living Word (Jesus Christ).   John 1:1-3,14

Read in connection with this the "Faith Chapter", Hebrews 11, and see how each of these faith heroes received a word from God.

Example: The manner in which Abraham manifests faith is the manner in which we must manifest faith (Hebrews 11:8-12; Romans 4:16-21).

1. He heard the Word.
2. Hope concerning the future was a result of his faith in the present.
3. He refused to accept the evidences of his senses.
4. He did not waiver in his commitment.
5. He rejoiced in the word as an accomplished fact.

Scriptural faith is a condition of the heart, not the mind. It is in the present, not only in the future. It produces a positive change in the behaviour and experience. It is based solely on God's Word and accepts the testimony of the senses only when it agrees with the text of God's Word. It is expressed by confession with the mouth. (Read Romans 10:8-13).

F. ARE THERE DIFFERENT LEVELS OF FAITH?

Yes, the Bible teaches that there are various levels or measures of faith.

1. God gives to every believer ——————————————————————
   Romans 12:3-6

2. Faith is likened to a seed. A seed has the potential to grow.

   Examples :

   * ——————————————————————— Matthew 6:30   3.
   * ——————————————————————— Matthew 8:10   2.
   * ——————————————————————— James 2:22   1.

G. IN RELATIONSHIP TO FAITH, HOW DO WE APPROPRIATE GOD'S WORD?

1. Receive the quickened promises in God's Word that applies to the need.
   Philippians 4:19; 2 Corinthians 1:20 *For all the promises of God in Him are yea, and in Him Amen, unto the glory of God by us.*

2. Fulfil all the conditions attached to that promise.
   Exodus 15:26; Isaiah 1:19-20; Psalm 37:5 *Commit your way unto the Lord; trust also in Him; and He shall bring it to pass.*

3. With patience accept the trying of your faith and God's testing of your faith in the Word.
   Hebrews 6:12-15; Psalm 105:19; James 1:3-4 *Knowing this, that the trying of your faith works patience. But let patience have her perfect work, that you may be perfect and entire, wanting nothing.*

4. We must firmly maintain faith unto the fulfilment of the promise (2 Peter 1:3-4). Our confession should always be in harmony with God's Word
   Hebrew 3:1; 1 John 5:14 *And this is the confidence that we have in Him, that if we ask anything according to His will, He hears us.*

5. Actively looking to Jesus is one of the keys to a victorious Christian life.
   Hebrews 12:2 *Looking unto Jesus, the Author and Finisher of our faith.*

6. Our faith cannot be based on **feelings**, but must be firmly based on **Scripture**.
   John 3:16; 1:12; Revelation 12:10-11; 1 John 1:9.

H. WHAT IS THE EVIDENCE OF THE NEW BIRTH?

How can one know that they are truly born again, born from above? It is through faith in the Word of God and the Spirit of God that a person receives the assurance of salvation.

In new birth one receives:

1. _____ Galatians 3:26.

2. _____ Galatians 4:6; 2 Peter 1:4.

3. _____ Ephesians 1:19; Acts 1:8

4. _____ Matthew 7:21; John 15:10.

5. _____ Romans 12:2; John 16:13.

6. _____ Philippians 4:6-7; John 14:27.

7. _____ Ephesians 2:10.

8. _____ Romans 8:28-29.

LESSON FOUR

WATER BAPTISM

Then those who gladly received his word were baptised ... (Acts 2:41).

Following what the writer to the Hebrew Christians said in Hebrews 6:1-2, the doctrine of baptisms is the next important step in the first principles of Christ.

Water baptism is not merely a ritual or a meaningless ceremony, but a definite experience in the life of a New Testament Christian, as recorded for us not only in the Gospels, but in the Acts of the Apostles and the Epistles (Acts 2:38-41; Romans 6:3-4).

A. WHAT IS THE MEANING OF THE WORD "BAPTISE"?

The Greek word *baptizo* means *to dip, to plunge, to immerse.* (Mark 1:5; John 3:23; Acts 8:36-39). By definition and usage, the word means:

_____

_____

B. WHY HAVE THE ORDINANCE OF WATER BAPTISM?

1. Jesus commanded it.   Mark 16:16; Matthew 28:16-20.
2. Jesus was baptised.   Matthew 3:13-17.
3. The Apostles commanded it.   Acts 2:37-47; Acts 10:44-48.
4. If we love Him, we will keep His commandments.   John 14:15.
5. We validate our faith by our obedience.   James 2:17-18.

C. WHO IS THE ORDINANCE FOR?

In every Scripture listed below it will be seen that people heard, believed and received the Word, and then were baptised.

_____ and _____ always preceded water baptism. Therefore it is a "believer's baptism".

1. "He that believes and is baptised..."   Mark 16:15-16.
2. The Samaritans believed and were baptised.   Acts 8:12-15.
3. The eunuch believed and was baptised.   Acts 8:35-38.
4. Peter commanded that the Gentiles be baptised.   Acts 10:47-48.
5. The Ephesian disciples believed and were baptised.   Acts 19:4-5.

Also read Acts 9:17-18; 16:30-34; 18:8.

Water baptism is an essential part of obedience; it is not optional. To refuse water baptism is to live in disobedience to the revealed Word of God.

NOTE: Water baptism involved a confession of faith in the Lordship of Christ. Acts 8:36-39; Romans 10:9-10. The prerequisites of baptism are repentance, faith and confession of sin. (These clearly exclude infant baptism).

D. WHAT IS THE SIGNIFICANCE OF WATER BAPTISM?

Water baptism is a real spiritual experience, yet symbolic. God was present at Jesus' baptism, and He is there when we are baptised, working by His Spirit. In baptism we are identified with Christ. We are baptised into Christ's:

1. _____ Romans 6:3,4,5,11.

2. _____ Colossians 2:12.

3. _____ Colossians 3:1; Romans 6:4-5.

Baptism is identification with Christ. In salvation we **accept** Christ's death, burial and resurrection. In baptism we **participate in** and are **identified with** His death, burial and resurrection.

1. By baptism we stand as "**dead**".

2. By immersion we **bury** the "dead".

3. By being raised up out of the water, we **rise** to walk in newness of life.

E. INTO WHAT NAME IS THE BELIEVER TO BE BAPTISED?

Jesus commanded His disciples to baptise *into the name of the Father, and of the Son, and of the Holy Spirit* (Matthew 28:19). These are not the **names**, but the **titles** of the three Persons of the Godhead. A study of the Gospels, the Acts and the Epistles on the subject of baptism reveals clearly into what **name** the people who repented and believed were baptised. Mark 16:15 shows that baptism was strictly for believers. So we need to look at the Scriptures to find out the name of the Father, the Son, and the Holy Spirit. Agur of old asked the crucial question, W*hat is His **name**, and His Son's **name**, if you can tell me?* (Proverbs 30:4).

1. WHAT IS THE NAME OF THE FATHER?

This (I AM, or the LORD) *is My Name forever and My memorial to all generations.* (Exodus 3:15).
The LORD is His Name. (Exodus 15:3).
I am the LORD, that is My Name. (Isaiah 42:8).
The LORD is His Name. (Jeremiah 33:2).
They shall know that My Name is the LORD. (Jeremiah 16:21; Amos 5:8; Psalm 83:18; Isaiah 12:2; James 1:17).

The Name **LORD** is used over 6800 times in the Old Testament. Not once did God declare that His name was **Father**. Father is a **title**, not a name.

2. WHAT IS THE NAME OF THE SON?

You shall call His Name JESUS. (Luke 1:31).
She shall bring forth a son and you shall call His Name Jesus. (Matthew 1:21).
His eternal name was **THE WORD**, but when the Word was made flesh, His human name was **JESUS**. (John 1:1-3,14-18; Revelation 19:13).

The name of **Jesus** is used approximately 1000 times in the New Testament.

3. WHAT IS THE NAME OF THE HOLY SPIRIT?

The Holy Spirit is also involved in the name of the Godhead at baptism. A study and interpretation of the name *Christ* actually shows that the Godhead, as Father, Son and Holy Spirit are each involved. This is seen in the following Greek words used in the New Testament.

* *Chrio* (Greek verb) = to anoint.
  The Father is the one who **anoints**. He is the anointer.
  (Luke 4:18; Acts 4:27; 10:38; Hebrew 1:9; 2 Corinthians 1:21).

* *Christos* (Greek noun) = the anointed one.
  The Son is the one who is **anointed**, or the anointed one.
  (John 1:41; Matthew 3:16; Isaiah 61:1-3; Luke 4:16-21; John 6:69; 20:31).

* *Chrisma* (Greek noun) = the anointing.
  The Holy Spirit is the one who is the anointing (1 John 2:20,27).
  The anointing abides within. This word *chrisma* is the Greek noun for anointing oil. The Holy Spirit is the Divine Oil, the anointing oil.

The *chrisma* (the anointing oil, the Holy Spirit) made Jesus the *christos* (the anointed one, the Messiah, the Christ). His name was known as **Jesus Christ** after His baptism, when the Holy Spirit descended upon Him and **remained** upon Him. It is in this way the name of the Holy Spirit is understood.

The disciples at Antioch were called *Christians*, being followers of the Anointed One, Jesus Christ (Acts 11:27). This showed that they were anointed by the Holy Spirit too.

Thus the name of the Father, the Son and the Holy Spirit all comes together in the name of the **LORD JESUS CHRIST**, the triune name for the triune God.

F. WHAT NAME IS CONNECTED WITH WATER BAPTISM IN THE ACTS AND THE EPISTLES?

A consideration of the references to baptism in the Acts and the Epistles shows that there was a clear connection with the name of the **Lord Jesus Christ** (see Acts 2:36-41; 8:12ff; 9:5; 10:48; 16:14ff; 18:8; 19:1-6; Romans 6:3-4; 1 Corinthians 1:10-17; Galatians 3:27; Ephesians 4:4; Colossians 2:12; James 2:7; 1 Peter 3:20-21). What we find in Acts and in the Epistles is the Apostles' obvious understanding of how they were to_____ the _____ given to them by Jesus in Matthew 28 and Mark 16.

G. WHAT FORMULA MAY BE USED IN WATER BAPTISM?

There are many ways to express the truths that we have studied in the Bible, and the following is a Biblically based formula which we use for water baptism.

To the person being baptised:
> **Upon confession of your faith,**
> **I baptise you into THE NAME of the Father,**
> **And of the Son, and of the Holy Spirit,**
> **Into THE NAME of the LORD JESUS CHRIST,**
> **And into the likeness of His death,**
> **That just as Christ was raised from the dead by the glory of the Father,**
> **even so you also shall rise to walk in newness of life.**

This formula is composed from three verses of Scripture:

1. **QUOTES** the Command of Jesus in the Gospel (Matthew 28:19).

2. **INVOKES** the Triune Name of the Lord Jesus Christ as used by the disciples in the Book of Acts, and

3. **DECLARES** the spiritual truth and significance of baptism in the Epistles (Romans 6:3-4).

SUMMARY:

Over the years, as Church history reveals, Christians have tried to reconcile the apparent discrepancy between the command of Jesus in the Gospels, and the administration of baptism in the Acts, and the teachings on baptism in the Epistles, many not having come up with satisfactory answers. As a result, formulas for water baptism have caused much dissension and division in the Church.

Particularly in regard to baptism, we need to recognise that no doctrine of Scripture can be built on one reference only, but all references should be brought together and compared, and then conclusions reached. We need to remember that Scripture interprets and complements Scripture. Therefore we conclude that when Jesus commanded us to baptise into the Name of the Father, and of the Son, and of the Holy Spirit, the name is understood and interpreted in the triune name of the **LORD JESUS CHRIST**. A triune name for a triune God!

In the light of the references to baptism in the Gospels, the Acts and the Epistles, we firmly believe that water baptism administered in the formula made up of the three Scriptures given just above is Biblically sound.

And this water symbolises baptism that now saves you also – not the removal of dirt from the body but the pledge of a good conscience towards God. It saves you by the resurrection of Jesus Christ. 1 Peter 3:21.

The following are the references, or brief quotes, to baptism in the Acts and the Epistles as taken from several translations (ie. A.V.: R.V.: Lamsa: Douav: Amp N.T.)

BAPTISM IN THE GOSPELS	BAPTISM IN THE ACTS	BAPTISM IN THE EPISTLES

1. The Command of Jesus (Matthew: 28:19. A.V.)
 	
Baptising them in The Name:
 	
    Of The Father.
    And of The Son.
    And of The Holy Spirit.
 	
Into The Name. R.V.
 	
2. Believer's Baptism (Mark 16:15. A.V.)
 	
He that *believes*, and is baptised, shall be saved
	1. Jerusalem – Acts 2:36-41 (Peter).
	Baptised in *The Name of Jesus Christ*. A.V.
	Baptised into *The Name of Jesus Christ*. R.V.
	Baptised in *The Name of the Lord Jesus*. L.
	Baptised in *The Name of the Jesus Christ*. D.
	
	2. Samaria – Acts 8:12-16; 35-38 (Philip).
	Baptised in *The Name of the Lord Jesus*. A.V., R.V. Into The Name of...
	L.D. (Note vs. 12 – Lamsa).
	
	3. Damascus – Acts 9:5-18; 22:16 (Ananias).
	Baptised, *calling on The Name of the Lord.* A.V. calling on *His Name*. R.V. D.
	calling on *The Name of the Lord.* L.
	
	4. Ceasarea – Acts 10:48 (Peter).
	Baptised in *The Name of the Lord.* A.V.
	Baptised in *The Name of Jesus Christ*. R.V.
	Baptised in *The Name of our Lord Jesus Christ*. L.
	Baptised in *The Name of our Lord Jesus Christ*. D.
	
	5. Philippi – Acts 16:14-15, 31-34 (Paul).
	Believe on the Lord Jesus Christ and be saved... and was baptised ... *believing in God.* A.V.
	
	6. Corinth – Acts 18:8 (Paul). 1 Corinthians 1:10-17.
	Believe on the Lord ... and were baptised A.V.
	Were ye baptised in the *name of Paul* ? A.V.
	
	7. Ephesus – Acts 19:1-6 (Paul).
	Baptised in *The Name of the Lord Jesus*. A.V. R.V.
	Baptised in *The Name of our Lord Jesus Christ*. L.
	Baptised in *The Name of the Lord Jesus Christ*. D.
		1. Romans – (Paul) – Romans 6:3-4.
		As many of us as were baptised *into Jesus Christ* were baptised into *His death* ... buried *with Him* by baptism. A.V.
		
		2. Corinthians – (Paul) – 1 Corinthians 1:10-17.
		Were ye baptised in *the Name of Paul?*
		Lest any should say I baptised in mine own name. A.V.
		Into the Name of Paul? R.V.
		All baptised *unto Moses.* A.V.
		Into Moses. R.V. 1 Corinthians 10:1-3.
		
		3. Galatians – (Paul) – Galatians 3:27.
		As many as were baptised *into* Christ.
		A.V. Those of us... baptised in *The Name of Christ....* L.
		
		4. Ephesians – (Paul) – Ephesians 4:4; Hebrews 6:2
		There is...*One Baptism* –)
		Doctrine of Baptisms –) Acts 19:5
		
		5. Colossians – (Paul) – Colossians 2:12.
		Buried *with Him* in baptism. A.V.
		
		6. The Twelve Tribes – (James) – James 2:7.
		That *worthy Name* by the which ye are *called.* A.V.
		The *precious Name* by which you are *distinguished and called (The Name of Christ invoked in Baptism.* Amp.N.T.)
		
		7. The Strangers – (Peter) – 1 Peter 3:20-21. A.V.
		The like figure whereunto Baptism doth also now save us, not the putting away of the filth of the flesh...but the answer of a good conscience toward God by the resurrection of Jesus Christ.

LESSON FIVE

HOLY SPIRIT BAPTISM

"and you shall receive the gift of the Holy Spirit..." (Acts 2:38)

In Hebrews 6:2, the writer talks about *baptisms*, that is, baptism in water and baptism in the Holy Spirit. Having looked at water baptism, we now turn to baptism in the Holy Spirit.

The outpouring of the Holy Spirit in the last days was foretold by Old Testament prophets as in Isaiah 32:15, 44:3; Joel 2:28-29; Ezekiel 11:19-20; 36:25-28. We are living in those last days that Joel spoke of, the age of the Holy Spirit. God's will is that everything in us as Christians and in the church be done by the ministry of the Holy Spirit.

A. WHERE DOES THE BIBLE TEACH THAT THE HOLY SPIRIT IS A PERSON?

1. The Holy Spirit is not just a force or influence. He is a person. Jesus referred to the Holy Spirit as *He*. (John 14:16-17, 15:26, 16:13-14).

2. Peter asked Ananias why he had lied to the Holy Spirit (Acts 5:3). He then said that he had lied to God. The Holy Spirit is God – the third **Person** in the Godhead.

3. The Holy Spirit has the following attributes of personality:

    (a) Intelligence   -Nehemiah 9:20.
    (b) Knowledge   -Acts 5:3-4; 1 Corinthians 2:9-11.
    (c) Mind   -Romans 8:27.
    (d) Will   -1 Corinthians 12:11.
    (e) Love   -Romans 15:30.
    (f) Grief   -Ephesians 4:30.

B. WHAT ARE SOME BIBLICAL SYMBOLS FOR THE HOLY SPIRIT?

These symbols describe the Holy Spirit and his various manifestations:

1. Fire   -Isaiah 4:4; Matthew 3:11; Acts 2:4.

2. Wind   -John 3:8; Acts 2:2-3.

3. Water   -John 7:38-39; 1 Corinthians 10:4.

4. Oil   -Psalm 89:20; Matthew 25:3; 1 John 2:27.

5. Dove   -Matthew 3:16.

C. HOW IS THE MINISTRY OF THE HOLY SPIRIT SEEN IN THE LIFE OF THE LORD JESUS CHRIST, THE HEAD OF THE CHURCH?

The Lord Jesus, as Head of the Church, had His whole life governed by the Holy Spirit. The Church, His Body, is also to be governed by the Holy Spirit, as the following two groupings of Scripture show.

CHRIST – THE HEAD		THE CHURCH – THE BODY
1. ————————	Luke 1:33-35	John 3:1-5; 1 Peter 1:22-23.
2. ————————	Luke 3:22; 4:1	Acts 1:8; 2:14; Ephesians 5:18.
3. ————————	Matthew 4:1	Luke 4:1; Romans 8:14.
4. ————————	Luke 4:14-18	1 Peter 1:11-12.
5. ————————	Matthew 12:28	Acts 8:5-7.
6. ————————	Acts 10:38	2 Corinthians 1:21; 1 John 2:27.
7. ————————	Hebrews 9:14	Romans 12:1-2.
8. ————————	Romans 8:11	Romans 8:2,13.
9. ————————	Acts 1:2	Acts 15:28-29.

D. IS "BAPTISM IN THE HOLY SPIRIT" A BIBLICAL TERM?

1. It was used:
    ❖ by John the Baptist (Matthew 3:11; John 1:30-33).
    ❖ by Jesus Himself (Acts 1:5).
    ❖ by the apostle Peter (Acts 11:16).

2. It is also spoken of as being:
    ❖ filled with the Spirit (Acts 2:1-4).
    ❖ the firstfruits of the Spirit (Romans 8:23).
    ❖ sealed with the Spirit (Ephesians 1:13).
    ❖ the earnest (guarantee, down payment, 'engagement ring', modern Greek) of the Spirit (Ephesians 1:14).
    ❖ the anointing of the Spirit (1 John 2:20,27; 2 Corinthians 1:27).

We should note that the New Testament takes for granted that every believer who follows the command of Jesus (Mark 16:17) and the Word of God received the baptism of the Spirit (Acts 2:38-39). The norm in the early church was that all who were exposed to the Gospel were filled with the Spirit. So the Bible does not offer great defences on the question, *"Do I have to receive the Holy Spirit and speak with tongues?"*

E. WHAT IS THE <u>INITIAL</u> EVIDENCE OF RECEIVING THE BAPTISM IN THE HOLY SPIRIT?

The initial sign and manifest evidence of receiving the baptism in the Holy Spirit in the New Testament was **speaking with other tongues**.

1. Jesus – *They shall speak with new tongues* (Mark 16:17).

2. Jerusalem – *They spoke with tongues* (Acts 2:1-4). The initial manifestation.

3. Samaria – What did Simon see and hear? (Acts 8:5-24).

4. Damascus – (Acts 9:17-19 with 1 Corinthians 14:18).

5. Caesarea – *They spoke with tongues* (Acts 10:44-48; 11:15-17). Normative evidence.

6. Corinth – (Acts 18:1-11 with 1 Corinthians 12:13-14).

7. Ephesus – *They spoke with tongues and prophesied* (Acts 19:1-7; Ephesians 1:13. Compare also Isaiah 28:11-12 with 1 Corinthians 14:21). Normative evidence.

F. WHAT IS THE PURPOSE OF SPEAKING IN TONGUES?

1. It is the initial sign of receiving the baptism in the Holy Spirit, as we have seen.

2. It enables us to speak directly to God beyond the limits of human language, in worship, singing, prayer and intercession (Acts 10:45-46; 1 Corinthians 14:2,16-18).

3. It builds us up in our faith (1 Corinthians 14:4,18; Ephesians 6:18; Jude 20).

4. It enables us to speak mysteries (1 Corinthians 14:26).

5. God gets the one member of our body that we cannot tame, the tongue, and tames it by causing us to speak in tongues, to praise Him (James 3:5-8).

6. It addresses our propensity to pride (Isaiah 28:11-12; 1 Corinthians 1:18ff).

7. It is a sign to believers (Mark 16:17; John 7:37-39; Acts 10:45-46).

8. It is a sign that Christ has risen, ascended, and rules today (Acts 2:33).

9. It indicates our allegiance to Christ's Lordship (Acts 2:4, 32-39).

G. HOW DO WE RECEIVE THE BAPTISM OF THE HOLY SPIRIT?

1. We must receive the gift of God by faith, not by works.
    Romans 10:17 says "This only would I learn of you. Received ye the Spirit by the works of the law, or by the hearing of faith?" (Galatians 3:2. See also verse 14).

2. A believer must come to the absolute conclusion that the baptism of the Holy Spirit is:

  (a) Biblical. (Acts 1:5,8; 8:17). Acts 2:4 reads "And they were filled with the Holy Spirit and began to speak with other tongues, as the Spirit gave them utterance."

  (b) Necessary (Ephesians 5:17-18).

  (c) Applicable for today (Mark 16:17; Acts 2:38).

  (d) Is an experience at or after salvation (Acts 8:12,14-17; 19:6).

  (e) Is evidenced by speaking in tongues (Acts 2:4; 10:44-46; 19:6; Mark 16:17).

  (f) Beneficial (Romans 8:26-27; 1 Corinthians 14:2,18,22). "But ye, beloved, building up yourselves on your most holy faith, praying in the Holy Ghost."

3. When we come to God to receive the gift of the Holy Spirit, we never need to fear receiving something other than what God promised (Luke 11:1-13).

  (a) What was Jesus teaching His disciples to do (11:1)? _____

  (b) What was the principle He taught them (11:11-13)? _____

  _____

4. We receive the Holy Spirit by:

  (a) Heart preparation, _____ (Acts 2:37-38).

  (b) Hearing the Word by faith and believing God's promise, nothing doubting (Luke 11:13; John 7:38-39).

  (c) _____, a great desire to receive, for *he that hungers shall be filled* (Matthew 5:6). *Draw near to God and He will draw near to you* (James 4:8).

  (d) _____ to receive (Luke 11:13).

  (e) _____ to receive. God keeps His promises.

  (f) Being prepared to receive the laying on of hands. In Acts the Lord also used the ministry of the laying on of hands (eg. Acts 8:14-17).

5. Relax in God's presence. You do not have to strive or work for the gift of the Holy Spirit. Work pays **wages**; baptism in the Holy Spirit is a **gift**. Just yield to God's will and accept the gift of the Spirit of God.

Note : The experience of "baptism" fulfils the Old Testament rite of circumcision, and becomes New Covenant circumcision, as seen in the following:

OLD TESTAMENT RITE	NEW TESTAMENT FULFILMENT
1. Ordinance involved blood-shed and circumcision of the flesh.	1. The body and blood of Jesus and circumcision of the heart.
2. The invocation of the name on the eighth day.	2. The invocation of the Godhead name and resurrection.
3. The sign and seal of the Abrahamic Covenant relationship.	3. The Holy Spirit is the sign and seal of the New Covenant relationship.

Read Genesis 17:1-4; Joshua 5:1-9 with Colossians 2:11-12; Philippians 2:2-3.

LESSON SIX

THE APOSTLES' DOCTRINE

"and they continued steadfastly in the apostles' doctrine..." (Acts 2:42)

As we come to this study, it is worth reminding ourselves that **everything** we do in life arises from our theology, whatever that theology is. The person bent on gratifying himself says, "Eat, drink and be merry, for tomorrow we die." Even how the atheist lives is determined by his theology. He will say, "There is no God; there is no judgement!" But that is not what the Bible has to say. The Christian will seek to live a life that is pleasing to the Lord. For that to be possible, he has to have a transformed value system (Romans 12:2). That takes place by conforming it to the teaching of the Bible (Philippians 4:8; 2 Timothy 3:16-17). Then the **lifestyle** will agree with the value system, and God will be well pleased.

A. IS IT IMPORTANT TO UNDERSTAND THE DOCTRINES OF THE BIBLE ?

Yes! It is very important to understand what God says in His Word. In Psalm 119, the Psalmist gives an extended exposition of the practical implications of God's Word for him. Jesus said, *You shall know the truth, and the **truth** shall set you free,* (John 8:32). Not only did He say that He is the truth, but also, *My doctrine is not Mine, but His who sent Me,* (John 7:16). In His prayer, He confessed, *Your word is truth,* (John 17:17).

The word "doctrine" means: _____

Ephesians 4:13-15, *till we all come to the unity of the faith and the knowledge of the Son of God, to a perfect man, to the measure of the stature of the fulness of Christ; that we should no longer be children, tossed to and fro and carried about with every wind of doctrine, by the trickery of men, in the cunning craftiness by which they lie in wait to deceive, but speaking the truth in love, may grow up in all things into Him, who is the head, – Christ.*

There are various doctrines mentioned in the Bible:

(a) The doctrine of _____ .
   Deuteronomy 32:2; Proverbs 4:2; Titus 2:10.

(b) The doctrine of _____ .
   John 7:16-17; 2 John 9-10; Hebrews 6:1-2.

(c) The doctrines of _____ .
   1 Timothy 4:1; Revelation 2:14-15,24.

(d) The doctrine of _____ .
   Mark 7:7; Ephesians 4:14; Matthew 16:12.

(e) The doctrine of _____ .
   Acts 2:42.

As Christians, it does matter **what** we believe. It also matters **how** we arrived at those beliefs. It is not good enough to accept at face value what anybody tells us. We need to check out the Bible for ourselves, using proper methods of study and interpretation so that we can make an informed conclusion on what the **Bible** teaches. (1 Timothy 4:6,13,16; 6:3-5; Titus 2:7-10).

Every religion, true and false, has its essential doctrines. When these are believed and practised they determine:

1. _____ – what we are

2. _____ – how we think

3. _____ – what we do

4. _____ – where we go.

That is why we need to be established in **Biblical** doctrines (2 Timothy 3:14-17; 1 Peter 3:15). We must hold fast the faithful word as we have been taught that we may be able by <u>sound doctrine</u> to exhort and to convince those who contradict and oppose (Titus 1:9), and we need to have a ready Biblical answer for those who have a genuine enquiry. We need to know **what** we believe and **why** we believe it, and **how** to communicate it.

Your Word is a lamp to my feet

And a light to my path.

Psalm 119:105.

B. WHAT ARE THE BASIC DOCTRINES OF _____ CHRISTIAN FELLOWSHIP?

While we recognise that God cannot be confined to articles of faith or doctrinal statements, we also realise that strange doctrines of men and demons are abounding today, as Paul predicted (1 Timothy 4:1). Therefore it is needful to provide a statement of faith which encapsulates what we believe as a local church to be the apostles' doctrine as recorded in the Bible. The following statement of faith can be found in our Constitution as well and sets out briefly the essential areas of Biblical doctrine.

STATEMENT OF FAITH

1. **We believe** in the plenary-verbal inspiration of the accepted canon of the Scriptures as originally given (2 Timothy 3:16; 1 Corinthians 2:13).
2. **We believe** in the eternal Godhead Who has revealed Himself as ONE God existing in THREE Persons; Father, Son and Holy Spirit; distinguishable but indivisible (Matthew 28:19; 2 Corinthians 13:14).
3. **We believe** in the creation, test and fall of man as recorded in Genesis; his total spiritual depravity and inability to attain to Divine righteousness (Romans 5:12,18).
4. **We believe** in the Lord Jesus Christ, the Saviour of men, conceived of the Holy Spirit, born of the virgin Mary, very God and very man (Luke 1:26-35; John 1:18; Isaiah 7:14, 9:6).
5. **We believe** Christ died for our sins, was buried and rose again the third day, and personally appeared to His disciples (1 Corinthians 15:1-4; Romans 4:24).
6. **We believe** in the bodily ascension of Jesus to heaven, His exaltation, and personal, literal and bodily coming again the second time for the Church (John 14:2-3; 1 Thessalonians 4:13-18).
7. **We believe** in the salvation of sinners by grace, through repentance and faith in the perfect and sufficient work of the cross of Calvary by which we obtain remission of sins (Ephesians 2:8-9; Hebrews 9:12,22; Romans 5:11).
8. **We believe** in the necessity of water baptism by immersion in the Name of the eternal Godhead in order to fulfil the command of Christ (Matthew 28:19; Acts 2:34-36; 19:1-6).
9. **We believe** in the baptism of the Holy Spirit as an experience at or subsequent to salvation, with the Scriptural evidence; namely, speaking in other tongues as the Spirit gives utterance (Acts 2:1-4; 8:14-17; 10:44-46; Galatians 3:14-15). For the 120 it was initial and in Acts speaking in tongues was normative.
10. **We believe** in the operation of the gifts of the Spirit as enumerated in 1 Corinthians 12-14, as manifested in the early Church.
11. **We believe** in the Spirit-filled life, a life of separation from the world and perfecting of holiness in the fear of God as an expression of Christian faith (Ephesians 5:18; 2 Corinthians 6:14; 7:1).
12. **We believe** in the healing of the body by Divine power, or Divine healing in its varied aspects as practised in the early Church (Acts 4:30; Romans 8:11; 1 Corinthians 12:9; James 5:14).
13. **We believe** in the table of the Lord, commonly called Communion or the Lord's Supper, for believers (1 Corinthians 11:28-32).
14. **We believe** in eternal life for believers (John 5:24; 3:16) and eternal punishment for unbelievers (Mark 9:43-58, 2 Thessalonians 1:9; Revelation 20:10-15).
15. **We believe** in the reality and personality of Satan and the eternal judgement of Satan and his angels (Matthew 25:41; Revelation 20:10-15).
16. **We believe** that there is one true universal Church, made up of genuine believers. However, this one universal Church is also composed of many local churches in given localities. These churches are under the sovereign headship of the Lord Jesus Christ, exercising autonomous government under Him, administering all its local affairs and ministry, as well as the propagation of the Gospel (Matthew 16:18; 18:15-20; Acts 15:22).

This STATEMENT OF FAITH shows that _____ Christian Fellowship is a Church that strongly believes in the essential BIBLICAL, FUNDAMENTAL, EVANGELICAL and CHARISMATIC doctrines.

LESSON SEVEN

PRAISE and WORSHIP

A. IS WORSHIP IMPORTANT?

Yes! (See Isaiah 61:3; Matthew 4:10; Revelation 1:6; Acts 24:14).

B. HOW ARE WE TO WORSHIP GOD?

(See John 4:20-24; 17:17; Mark 7:7-9; Psalm 9:1; 111:1).

1. Worship in —————————————

2. Worship in —————————————

C. WHAT DOES WORSHIP SIGNIFY?

(See 2 Chronicles 29:11; 1 Peter 2:5; Revelation 1:6; Romans 12:1; Hebrews 13:15-16).

A believer is a _____ to God to offer _____

_____

D. WHEN ARE WE TO WORSHIP?

1. _____ Psalm 34:1.

2. _____ Psalm 35:27.

3. _____ Psalm 146:1-3.

4. _____ Psalm 104:33; 146:2.

E. WHERE ARE WE TO WORSHIP?

1. In our——————————— Psalm 149:5.

2. In the——————————— Psalm 22:22; 35:18; 100:2,4; 134:12; 135:2.

3. In the_____ before the _____ Acts 16:25-34; Psalm 40:3.

F. WHY SHOULD WE WORSHIP?

1. God has ordained and requires it (Isaiah 60:18; 62:7; Psalm 100:4).

2. God inhabits our praises. They make a throne for Him (Psalm 22:3).

3. It glorifies God (Psalm 50:23).

4. It is the voice of God speaking to His people (Jeremiah 33:11; Psalm 102:13-18).

5. Worship changes us to His image (Psalm 106:19-20; 115:8; Romans 1:21-23).

6. God meets with us as we worship Him (Exodus 29:41-42; 2 Chronicles 5:13; 15:14; 20:19-21).

G. IN WHAT WAYS ARE WE TO WORSHIP THE LORD ?

1. _____

   O come, let us sing to the LORD! Let us shout joyfully to the rock of our salvation.
   (Psalm 95:1. See also Psalm 81:1; 66:8; 42:4; 149:6; 55:17; 32:11).

2. _____

   _____   *O clap your hands all you peoples.* (Psalm 47:1; 98:8).

   _____   *Lift up your hands in the sanctuary, and bless the Lord.*

   (Psalm 134:3. Also Psalm 141:2).

   _____ *(Psalm 150:3-6).*

3. _____

   _____   *Behold, bless ye the Lord, all ye servants of the LORD, who by*
   night stand in the house of the Lord. (Psalm 134:1).

   _____*O come, let us worship and bow down: Let us kneel before the*
   LORD our maker. (Psalm 95:6).

   _____*Let them praise His name in the dance: Let them sing praises*
   unto Him with the timbrel and harp. (Psalm 149:8. Also Psalm 150:4; Acts 3:1-11).

CONCLUSION

There should be times of praise and worship. The congregation should be both a <u>praising</u> and <u>worshipping</u> people. Praise is the expression of thanks, gratitude, adoration and applause for the goodness of God, both to God as well as to others. Worship is pouring out our inner selves to the Lord in unashamed affectionate love and devotion.

But the time is coming and is already here, when by the power of God's Spirit people will worship the Father as He really is, offering Him the true worship that He wants. God is Spirit, and only by the power of His Spirit can people worship Him as He really is (John 4:23-24).

LESSON EIGHT

FELLOWSHIP

"They continued steadfastly in the apostle's doctrine and in fellowship... " (Acts 2:42).
"But if we walk in the light as He is in the light, we have fellowship with one another, and the blood of Jesus Christ His Son cleanses us from all sin." (1 John 1:7).

A. WHAT IS FELLOWSHIP?

1. A Greek word often used in the New Testament is *koinonia*, from which two main words are translated in our English Bible:

   (a) **Fellowship**]

   ]   meaning, "the act of using a thing in common".

   (b) **Communion**]

2. The meaning of the words:

   (a) **Fellowship**: companionship; mutual sharing; gathering of people having the same interests; sharing life with another person.

   (b) **Communion**: to have in common; to share by all; participation, partnership.

B. WITH WHOM ARE WE TO FELLOWSHIP?

Fellowship must be in two directions to be effective – Godward, and manward.

1. **GODWARD** – Fellowship **vertically**.

   Our fellowship is with:

   _____ 1 John 1:3.

   _____ 1 Corinthians 1:9; 1 John 1:3.

   _____ Philippians 2:1.

   This fellowship is expressed in worship, praise and prayer. It is worship in spirit and in truth.

2. **MANWARD** – Fellowship **horizontally**.

   Our fellowship is with:

   _____ 1 John 1:7.

   _____ 2 Corinthians 8:4b.

   Believers also give and receive the right hand of fellowship (Galatians 2:9).
   True Christian fellowship is expressed both spiritually and practically.

(a) **Spiritually**: Acts 2:42-47 (Corporately in the temple)

1. Praying together.
2. Singing, praising and worshipping together.
3. Sharing together in testimony, exhortation, encouragement; building up one another through gifts of the Spirit.
4. Ministry of the Word; apostles' doctrine.
5. Communion; breaking of bread.

(b) **Practically**: Acts 2:44-46 (In the home)

1. Meeting together in houses or homes. Cell meetings. (Acts 2:46).
2. Meeting physical/material needs (Acts 2:45; 4:35).
3. To communicate; sharing with others (Hebrews 13:16).
4. Distributing to the necessity of the saints (Romans 12:13).
5. Hospitality (Romans 12:13).
6. Getting to know and appreciate each other. Visitation. (James 1:27).

Fellowship becomes the way of life in God's family. There is joy in really sharing and meeting spiritual, practical and social needs of our brothers and sisters in Christ.

C. WITH WHOM AND WHAT MUST WE NOT FELLOWSHIP?

1. The _____ - Ephesians 5:11; Psalm 94:20.
2. Satanic _____ - 1 Corinthians 10:18-20; Psalm 115:1-8.
3. _____ - 2 Corinthians 6:14.
4. _____ - 2 Peter 2; Jude 4,19; Romans 16:17.
5. _____ - 2 John 9-11; Galatians 1:7-10; 2 Timothy 3:1ff.
6. Disorderly _____ - Matthew 18:15-17; 1 John 1:7; 2:10-11;

2 Thessalonians 3:6. See also Titus 3:10-11; 2 Thessalonians 3:14;
1 Corinthians 15:33.

(a) Covetous – Inordinately desirous, greedy.

(b) Idolater – Inordinately fond of a person or thing.

(c) Railer – Abusive language, scornful.

(d) Drunkard – One who habitually drinks.

(e) Extortioner – To obtain from a person by oppression, or abuse of authority.

(f) Fornicator – Illicit sexual relationships.

<u>Do not eat with them</u> ...   <u>Do not keep company with them</u>.

LESSON NINE

COMMUNION, THE LORD'S TABLE

"...and in the breaking of bread..." Acts 2:42,46

In Matthew 26:26-29 Jesus instituted the Lord's Supper. We need to understand the Table of the Lord, to receive the benefit from it, both individually and also as the Body of Christ. In this study we look at the Lord's Table and how it is related to the life of the Church.

A. WHAT ARE SOME NAMES GIVEN TO COMMUNION?

1. _____ 1 Corinthians 11:20.

2. _____ 1 Corinthians 10:21.

3. _____ 1 Corinthians 10:16.

4. _____ Matthew 26:27; 15:36.

(Greek: "thanksgiving". SC2168, "The Eucharist")

B. WHO INSTITUTED THE COMMUNION?

1. The Lord Jesus instituted this meal with His disciples at the Feast of Passover (Matthew 26:17-19; Mark 14:12-26; Luke 22:1,7-8,15-20).

2. The Lord Jesus also gave particular revelation to Paul about communion, *For I have received from the Lord that which I also delivered to you, that the Lord Jesus on the same night in which He was betrayed took bread...* (Read 1 Corinthians 11:23).

C. WHAT ARE THE SYMBOLS USED IN COMMUNION?

1. Table.   1 Corinthians 10:21; Luke 22:30.

2. Bread.   1 Corinthians 10:16; Luke 22:19.

3. The fruit of the vine.   1 Corinthians 10:16; Luke 22:17-20.

D. WHAT IS THE SIGNIFICANCE OF THE SYMBOLS?

1. Table: Is a place of love and fellowship.
            (Leviticus 24:5-9; Psalm 23:5; Revelation 3:20).

2. Bread: _____ Matthew 26:2.

          _____ 1 Corinthians 10:16-17.

3. Fruit of the vine: _____ Matthew 26:27; 1 Corinthians 11:25).

E. WHAT ARE SOME OLD TESTAMENT EXAMPLES OF COMMUNION?

1. Abraham received communion. (Genesis 14:18).

2. The body and blood of the Passover lamb pointed to the Table of the Lord. (Exodus 12; Mark 14:12).

3. The table of bread in the Tabernacle of Moses. (Leviticus 24:5-9; Numbers 28:7; Exodus 25:23-30).

F. WHAT ARE SOME ESSENTIAL ATTITUDES IN COMING TO THE LORD'S TABLE?

1. Come to the table with a desire to **participate**. (Luke 22:14-15).

2. Come in **faith** believing. (Hebrews 11:6; Romans 14:23).

3. Come **remembering** (memorial). (1 Corinthians 11:24-25).

4. Come with **thanksgiving**. (Luke 22:17).

5. Come as a **Body**. (1 Corinthians 10:17).

6. Come **partaking together**. (1 Corinthians 11:33).
   (a) "The bread which we break"
   (b) "The cup which we bless"
   The cup of blessing which we bless, is it not the communion of the blood of Christ?
   The bread which we break, is it not the communion of the body of Christ?
   (1 Corinthians 10:16).

Jesus our great High Priest instituted Communion; we as priests partake together. Communion is an act of **sharing** and Christians obey the Scriptures as they break bread and drink the cup with each other. (Acts 2:46-47 Amplified Bible).

G. WHAT DO WE CELEBRATE IN COMMUNION?

1. _____
2. _____
3. _____

H. WHAT CAN WE EXPECT TO RECEIVE FROM COMMUNION?

1. For the worthy: _____ Matthew 15:25-26.

   _____ John 6:53-58.

2. For the unworthy: _____ 1 Corinthians 11:23-24.

   _____

As we understand this lesson, we will be able to properly discern (to have insight and perceive) the Lord's Table.

LESSON TEN

CHRISTIAN STEWARDSHIP

"... as good stewards of the manifold grace of God." 1 Peter 4:10.

In this study we will look at the meaning of Christian stewardship and how it relates to us as believers in the Lord Jesus Christ.

Stewardship is the systematic and proportionate giving of time, abilities and material possessions based on the conviction that these are a trust from God to be used in His service for the benefit of His kingdom. It is a **lifestyle**; recognising that God owns our person, our powers, our possessions, and using these faithfully to advance Christ's Kingdom in this world.

A. WHAT IS THE DIFFERENCE BETWEEN OWNERSHIP AND STEWARDSHIP?

1. Ownership – God is the owner of all things (Genesis 14:19-22; Psalm 24:1; 50:1-12; 68:19; 89:11; Haggai 2:8).

2. Stewardship – We are not owners, but we are responsible and accountable to use what we have been given in trust (Matthew 25:14-30; Luke 19:11-26).

GOD	MAN
The Giver	The Receiver
Possessor	Steward
The Owner	Responsible, accountable, privileged
	May use, or abuse and lose
The Rewarder	The rewarded faithful

B. WHAT ARE THE DIFFERENT OWNER-STEWARD RELATIONSHIPS?

1. _____ What you have received.
   Genesis 1:27; Acts 17:25; James 1:17.

2. _____ What you are allotted.
   Proverbs 24:30-34; Psalm 90:12; Ephesians 5:15-16.

3. _____ What you have been given to use.
   Matthew 25:14-30.

4. _____ What is entrusted to you.
   Haggai 2:8; Matthew 6:19-21; Colossians 3:1-2.

5. _____ What you labour for.
   Haggai 2:8; 1 Corinthians 16:1-2.

C. WHAT ARE THE REQUIREMENTS OF A GOOD STEWARD?

1. Faithfulness	1 Corinthians 4:1-2.
2. Teachable spirit	Psalm 27:11.
3. Desire to serve people	Romans 12:10-13.
4. Servant's heart	Galatians 5:13.
5. Willingness to give	Luke 6:38.

D. ARE STEWARDS ACCOUNTABLE?

Yes! The parable of the unjust steward teaches accountability. (Luke 16:1-3).

1. What was the steward accused of in verse 1? _____

2. What did the master do in verse 2? _____

3. Is it possible to forfeit our stewardship – verses 2-3? _____

4. Why was the steward commended in verse 8? _____

5. What is the real lesson for us in this parable? _____

_____

Note: The rich man called his steward to account for wasting his goods, or squandering on himself that with which he had been entrusted!

The steward's master did not commend the steward for his wrong and unjust actions he took with his creditors. He commended him for his **shrewdness** in how he handled unrighteous mammon. The real lesson to us here is that **faithfulness** is required of a steward, and that faithfulness in little qualifies for being entrusted with greater things.

We, as believers, are accountable to God for all the things that He entrusts to us. All that we are and all that we have comes from Him, and we are required as stewards to be faithful to Him in the way we use these things.

(Read Psalm 50:7-15,23).

"And you shall remember the LORD your God, for it is He who gives you power to get wealth..." (Deuteronomy 8:18).

Having established the fundamental principle that God is the OWNER of all things and that we are STEWARDS, accountable to God for all He has given us, this study considers what the Bible says about that which God entrusts to us financially, and our response to Him in **tithes and offerings** (Romans 12:1; 1 Corinthians 6:19-20).

E. WHAT IS THE NEW TESTAMENT TEACHING ABOUT FINANCES?

1. The Gospels contain more warnings against money and its misuse than any other subject.

2. About one in every four verses in Matthew, Mark and Luke deals with money.

3. About one in every six verses in the New Testament as a whole deals with or makes reference to money in some way.

4. Almost half of the parables of Jesus have reference to money in one way or another; particularly warning against covetousness.

5. The first disciple to fall was Judas. It was because of the **love** of money. He sold Jesus Christ for the price of a slave! (Matthew 26:14-16; 27:3-10; John 12:4-8; 13:27; Acts 1:25).

6. The first sin in the early church concerned the giving of money to the Lord. Satan infiltrated the glory of the early church through the love of money, when the spirit of giving was on the people. (Acts 4:32-5:10).

7. The sin of **simony** concerns money and seeking to buy the gift of God with it. (Acts 8:14-24).

8. Two of the New Testament words whose Greek numerical value equals 666, the number of the world system, are wealth and tradition. There is a time coming in which the power to buy or sell is connected with 666. (Revelation 13:16-18).

F. WHAT WARNING DOES THE NEW TESTAMENT GIVE CONCERNING MONEY?

Money is not evil in itself; money is neither moral nor immoral. The New Testament cautions us that it is the **love** of money that is the root of all evil. (Read 1 Timothy 6:6-11).

G. WHAT DOES THE BIBLE TEACH ABOUT TITHES AND OFFERINGS?

1. We are to bring our tithes and offerings to God's storehouse. (Malachi 3:7-12).

2. The storehouse is that place where the people of God are fed. (Nehemiah 10:38).

3. Tithes are used to support full-time ministry. (Numbers 18:21).

H. IS TITHING FOR TODAY?

Yes. The Old and New Testaments confirm the truth that believers are to give a tithe (one tenth) of their income.

1. Tithing **BEFORE** the Law

   (a) Abraham (covenant man) tithed to Melchisedek (Genesis 14:18-20).

   (b) Jacob (covenant man) made his vow to give a tenth at Bethel, which means *House of God.* (Genesis 28:22).

2. Tithing **UNDER** the Law – a LEGAL giver gives because he **has** to.
   Israel under the Mosaic Covenant. (Leviticus 27:30-33; Numbers 18:20-24,25-32).

3. Tithing under **GRACE** - a LOVING giver gives because s/he **loves** to.
   Jesus confirmed tithing. Tithing was not of the Law, but **before** the Law. (Matthew 23:23; Luke 11:42; 18:12; Hebrews 7:1-21).

I. WHAT IS THE DISTINCTION BETWEEN TITHES AND OFFERINGS?

OR, DO THE SCRIPTURES MAKE A DIFFERENCE BETWEEN TITHES AND OFFERINGS?

Yes! Tithes are the first 10% of our increase, whereas offerings are over and above the tithes.

"Will a man rob God? Yet you have robbed Me. But you say, Wherein have we robbed Thee? <u>In tithes and offerings.</u> You are cursed with a curse: For you have robbed Me, even this whole nation. Bring you all the tithes into the storehouse, that there may be meat in Mine house, and prove Me now herewith, says the Lord, if I will not open you the windows of heaven, and pour you out a blessing, that there shall not be room enough to receive it."
Malachi 3:8-10.

1. The Tithe, literally one tenth, is **God's** portion of our increase. It is not the leftovers; it is the **first part, the firstfruits**. When this is given to the LORD, He promises to stretch the rest to meet our needs. God can do far more with the 90% than we can with the 100%! (Read Proverbs 3:9-10).

   The tithe is not ours to give as offerings; it **already** belongs to God. If a believer pays tithes only and no offerings, he is not giving anything to God; he is only paying what is God's portion anyway. God says in His Word, *prove me now in this* (Malachi 3:8-10).

2. Offerings are over and above tithing. They are given as a response of love and gratitude to God. He knows that where we spend our money is an indication of where our heart is (Matthew 6:21). In any area of life, God never forces us against our will. So also with offerings. He wants our offerings to be free-will offerings, coming from overflowing hearts that are in love with the Lord. (Read Mark 12:41-44; 2 Corinthians 9:6-15).

CONCLUSION

The New Testament details the attitude and true spirit of giving (2 Corinthians 8 and 9).

LESSON ELEVEN

CHURCH MEMBERSHIP

"Now you are the body of Christ, and members in particular." 1 Corinthians 12:27

"The Lord added to the church daily those that were being saved." Acts 2:47

Every true Christian, at some time or another, must consider the issue of what it means to belong to the local church. In this study, we will look at what the Scriptures have to say on this area.

The apostle Paul used the human body and its members as one of the greatest illustrations of relationship in the Body of Christ, not only relating one with another, but the contribution of the individual member to the welfare of the whole body. (See 1 Corinthians 12:12-27 and Ephesians 4:16).

A. WAS A RECORD OF MEMBERSHIP KEPT IN THE EARLY CHURCH?

The Gospels and the Book of Acts imply that there was some definite church membership. The disciples of Jesus and the early believers were actually numbered and accounted for. Here are some examples.

1. Jesus chose 12 apostles, who were named and numbered (Luke 9:1-2).

2. Jesus later chose 70 others as His disciples and He sent them out (Luke 10:12).

3. Over 500 brethren saw Jesus in His ascension. They were known to Paul and to the early church (1 Corinthians 15:3-8).

4. Before Pentecost 120 disciples gathered in the upper room (Acts 1:15).

5. The *number* of the *names* was about 120.

6. At and after Pentecost multitudes were brought to Christ and into the church which Jesus said He would build.

7. There were added to them (the 120) about 3000 souls (Acts 2:41,47).

8. The number of men who believed were about 5000 (Acts 4:4).

9. The number of the disciples multiplied greatly in Jerusalem (Acts 6:7).

10. At least 10,000 believers were numbered in these Scriptures.

B. HOW DO YOU BECOME A MEMBER OF CHRIST'S CHURCH?

There are two aspects to church membership in the Book of Acts.

1. **Spiritual Membership** :
   One cannot **join** Christ's church, as one would join a club, etc. (Acts 5:1).
   In the early church, the members were first **added** (Greek ; *prostithemi* – to put to, to add, or to place beside) to the **Lord**. (Acts 5:14; 11:24).

   One must be **joined** in the Spirit, by the Spirit, **to the Lord** to be added to the Church, universal and spiritual. This is of first and primary importance.

2. **Practical Membership** :
   There must also be a visible and practical expression of church membership as seen in Acts. This is demonstrated in being a member of the local church. (See Acts 2:41,47).

   (a) Added to the **Lord** (spiritual) – Acts 5:14;11:24.
   (b) Added to **them** (physical) – Acts 2:41.
   (c) Added to the **church** (local) – Acts 2:47.

   One can easily become a member in any local church or denomination, but one must be **added to the Lord** first, that is, become born again, to belong to the true church. Otherwise we do not belong to Christ's body, and local church membership ultimately means nothing. On the other hand, it is not enough just to claim membership of the universal Body of Christ. The **practical expression** of membership of the universal church, or the Body of Christ is demonstrated in being **added** to a New Testament local church.

Acts 2:37-38 lays down the standard evidences for New Testament Church membership. These have never changed – in God's mind! These evidences were tangible and visible.

C. IS IT SCRIPTURAL TO HAVE SOME KIND OF CHURCH ROLL?

Yes! Old Testament and New Testament refer to books where the names of God's people were kept for records. It would be impossible to take care of God's sheep fully if no-one knew who they were or where they were, or if they really belonged to this or some other local church. Here are some examples of records in the Bible.

1. **Old Testament** :

   (a) The Israelites had their names in the Book of Genealogy of the Nation.
   They were **numbered before the Lord** (Numbers 1-2).
   (b) The Levites were also **numbered before the Lord** before they could minister in the priestly office (Numbers 3).
   (c) Every one **numbered** in Israel had to be redeemed with silver (Exodus 30:11-16).
   (d) The remnant from Babylon had to be **registered in the book** in order to minister in the priesthood (Ezra 63; Nehemiah 7).

2. **New Testament :**

(a) The Church of the Firstborn have their **names written in heaven** (Hebrews 12:22-24).

(b) The redeemed of all ages have their **names** also **written in the Book of Life** (Philippians 4:3; Revelation 13:8; 17:8; 20:12-15; 21:27).

God clearly keeps records! He has the names and numbers of the saints in His roll. God knows who is in His book and who is not. If God Himself does this, then there should be no problem if we as the Body of Christ do the same!

Note: Legal requirements stipulate that proper records of membership be kept in relation to church funds, holding of property, taxes, etc. This cannot be just an invisible, mystical method of record-keeping!

D. WHY DO SOME PEOPLE AVOID OR REJECT PRACTICAL CHURCH MEMBERSHIP?

1. Fear of being hurt.

2. Legalism.

3. Do not believe it is Scriptural.

4. Not submissive in spirit.

5. Desire to be self-governing, self-directing, lawless.

6. Unwilling to support the church financially with tithes and offerings.

7. Do not desire to come under correction, discipline or protection.

8. Do not want to be committed to anything local or visible.

9. Does not believe that God sets believers in the Body (Church) as it pleases Him (1 Corinthians 12:18).

E. WHAT ARE SOME RESPONSIBILITIES OF BEING A COMMITTED MEMBER?

1. Not neglecting to **meet together** for praise, worship, prayer, teaching of the Word, and building one another up (Hebrews 10:25).

2. Living a **consistent Christian life** (Galatians 5:16-26; Ephesians 4:1-8,22-32).

3. Being established in the **Apostles' doctrine** (Acts 2:42; Hebrews 5:11-13; 6:1-2).

4. Being **under the ministry and oversight** that Christ has set in His church (Ephesians 4:9-16; Hebrews 13:7,17; 1 Peter 5:1-5). Being prepared to receive discipline, correction and adjustment from the oversight as it is needed.

5. Exercising the authority of Christ by using the **keys of the Kingdom** (Matthew 16:18-19; Colossians 3:15 etc.)

6. Receiving, encouraging, exhorting and admonishing the other members of the fellowship (Romans 15:5-7; Ephesians 5:18-21; Hebrews 3:13; 10:24; Romans 15:14; Colossians 3:16-17; 2 Thessalonians 3:15). That is, ministering to one another, **serving one another**.

7. Maintaining the **unity of the Spirit** in the bond of peace (Ephesians 4:3; Colossians 3:14. Compare Proverbs 6:19).

8. Obeying the Great Commission of the Lord Jesus Christ in **reaching the lost** (Matthew 28:19-20).

F. WHAT ARE SOME BLESSINGS OF BEING A COMMITTED MEMBER?

1. Belonging to and being identified with a local body, where the true implications of **fellowship** can be worked out in corporate life. A New Covenant relationship.

2. The leadership, by God's grace, commit themselves to the **spiritual welfare and protection** of the members; practical care and concern (Ephesians 4:9-16).

3. **Security** in the family of God. As a child knows security in the natural family, so the children of God learn security in His family.

4. **Protection** from wolves who would otherwise come in to tear apart and destroy (Ezekiel 22:27; Matthew 7:15; Acts 20:28-32; 2 Peter 2:1).

5. Consistent food and **nourishment** from God's Word; balanced spiritual diet.

6. **Discipline** (Hebrews 12:5-13) **correction and adjustment** in the Christian life where it is needed (Galatians 6:1; 1 Thessalonians 5:12-14; Titus 2:1-10).

7. Support of the church's ministry by **tithes and offerings**, with the result that God opens the windows of heaven to pour out **His blessing** (Malachi 3:8-11; 2 Corinthians 9:6-12).

8. Receiving life through **the ministry of other members** of the Body (Ephesians 4:16; James 5:14 etc.)

9. Receiving life through the **Communion table**, and discerning the Body (1 Corinthians 11:17-34).

Although an adherent to the local church is cared for by the leadership, one cannot expect to receive **all** the **blessings and benefits** of the Lord's church when one is not willing to be committed to the **responsibilities** of membership. Commitment to the responsibilities of church membership opens the door to receiving and partaking in all the blessings of membership.

G. WHAT ABOUT CHURCH CONSTITUTIONS?

Because the believer is a citizen of "two worlds", that of a heavenly country and an earthly country, he is therefore required by the authority of Scriptures to live accordingly as a Christian citizen. This involves the government both Scripturally and legally.

1. SCRIPTURAL CONSITUTION

As far as the Christian citizen is concerned, the Scriptures alone are the one and only constitution by which he lives and to which he submits as a believer. God's laws and by-laws and His form of government for His church are laid out therein.

God's government of the church is that of apostles, prophets, evangelists, shepherds, teachers, elders, deacons and other leaders (Philippians 1:1 with Ephesians 4:9-16), and these together rule and serve the congregation, the Church. The Bible is the final court of appeal for all matters of Christian faith and conduct.

2. LEGAL CONSTITUTION

However, these same Scriptures teach the Christian citizen that he is to obey the powers that exist which are ordained by God. This involves civil government (Romans 13). These government rulers are the ministers of God also. Therefore, a Christian is called to submit himself to the ordinances of His government as long as they do not violate the government and law of the Kingdom of God (1 Peter 2:13-17).

Jesus told us to *render to Caesar the things that are Caesar's* (Matthew 22:17-21). Paul also confirmed this and told us to *render to all their dues; tribute to whom tribute is due; custom to whom custom; fear to whom fear; honour to whom honour* (Romans 13:7-8).

For fuller details, refer to "sample" constitution for membership at the appendix to these lessons.

ENCOURAGE ONE ANOTHER

LESSON TWELVE

LOCAL CHURCH GOVERNMENT

The Bible clearly identifies three main areas of government in society:
- Home Government
- Civil Government
- Church Government

See 1 Corinthians 11:1-3; Romans 13; Hebrews 13:7,17. In this study we will concentrate on church government. 1 Corinthians 12:28.

A. WHY IS THERE A NEED FOR GOVERNMENT?

Without government there would be lawlessness, anarchy and disorder. (See Judges 17:6; 21:25; 2 Thessalonians 2:3-4; 2 Peter 2:10).

B. WHAT FORM OF CHURCH GOVERNMENT IS USED IN THE NEW TESTAMENT?

The New Testament reveals that the church was governed by divinely appointed and anointed ministries, that is, apostles, prophets, evangelists, pastors and teachers, along with elders and deacons (Ephesians 4:9-16; Philippians 1:1).

The general consensus among Pentecostal churches is that all of the fivefold ascension gift ministers are elders (eg. 1 Peter 5:1) but not all elders are fivefold ministers.

It needs to be recognised that the fivefold ministry described in Ephesians 4:11 are all elders with oversight authority. The **names** given to them are not their titles, but describe their distinctive function in the body of Christ.

The simplest way to call these ministers and elders as a group is the *elders* or *the Eldership*.

C. DOES THE BIBLE TEACH PLURALITY OF ELDERSHIP IN THE LOCAL CHURCH?

Yes! In relation to local churches the word for *elder* is always in the plural (Acts 14:19-23).

1. Acts 14:23 —————————————————————
2. Acts 15:4-23 ————————————————————
3. Acts 16:4 ——————————————————————
4. Acts 20:17———————————————————————
5. Acts 21:17-18 ——————————————————
6. 1 Timothy 5:1,17-21 ————————————————

7. James 5:14 ——————————————————————

8. 1 Peter 5:1——————————————————————

9. Titus 1:5-11——————————————————————

10. Hebrews 13:17——————————————————————

D. WHAT ARE THE QUALIFICATIONS OF AN ELDER?

1 Timothy 3:1-7 and Titus 1:5-9 show the moral, domestic and spiritual qualifications required of those who are elders in the church.

E. WHAT IS THE BIBLICAL DEFINITION OF THE OFFICE OF A DEACON?

Translated *deacon* 3 times (eg. 1 Timothy 3:3-8; Philippians 1:1).
minister 20 times (eg. Mark 10:43-45).
servant 7 times (eg. Mark 9:35).

The word *deacon* means a *minister* or *servant*. In relation to the church, the deacons are involved in serving the people of God.

F. WHAT ARE THE QUALIFICATIONS OF A DEACON?

Acts 6:3 and 1 Timothy 3:8-11 show the moral, spiritual and domestic qualifications of a deacon.

G. WHAT IS THE FUNCTION OF THE FIVEFOLD ASCENSION-GIFT MINISTRIES?

This is a very brief description of the function and work of each of the fivefold ascension-gift ministries of apostles, prophets, evangelists, shepherds and teachers.

1. An Apostle
   - ❖ Lays foundational truths (Ephesians 2:20).
   - ❖ Establishes new churches (1 Corinthians 9:1-2).
   - ❖ Is humble and sacrificial (Philippians 2:1-4).
   - ❖ Is a spiritual instructor and father (1 Corinthians 4:15-16).

2. A Prophet
   - ❖ Lays foundational truths with the apostles (Ephesians 2:20).
   - ❖ Brings Divine illumination (Ephesians 3:3-5).
   - ❖ May foretell future events (Acts 11:27-28).
   - ❖ Exhorts, confirms and counsels (Acts 15:32).

3. An Evangelist
   - ❖ Has a ministry to the lost and the sick (Acts 8:5-8).
   - ❖ Is diligent in the Word (2 Timothy 2:15; 4:1-5).
   - ❖ Equips the saints to evangelise (Ephesians 4:11-12).

4. A Pastor
   - Tends and Cares for God's flock (Ezekiel 34:12-16).
   - Discerns and protects the flock from false ministers (Revelation 2).
   - Lays down his life for the sheep (John 10).
   - Feeds the flock on the Word of God (Ezekiel 34:1-2; Jeremiah 23:1-2).
     Note the plight of the false shepherds in verses quoted above.

5. A Teacher
   - Builds upon the foundations laid by apostles and prophets to
   - Establish the saints in God's Word (1 Corinthians 3).
   - Brings illumination of the revelation by inspiration (ie. opens the Scriptures) (Luke 24:44-45).
   - Jesus also taught, using miracles as **signs** (Luke 5:1-10).

H. WHAT IS THE FUNCTION OF THE FIVEFOLD MINISTRY AND THE ELDERSHIP?

There are three main words used in the New Testament which refer to one and the same person. These are seen in the following verses of the Bible.

Paul called the **elders** of the church of Ephesus to *"take heed to yourselves and to all the flock, over which the Holy Spirit has made you **overseers to shepherd** the church of God"* (Acts 20:17,28-32).

Peter wrote, *"The **elders** who are among you I exhort, I who am a fellow elder ... **Shepherd** the flock of God which is among you, serving as **overseers**"* (1 Peter 5:1. See also Titus 1:5-7).

To conclude from the New Testament:

1. **Elder**
   (Greek: *presbuteros*) which means *senior*, as used in reference to the Church in contrast to *novice*.

2. **Bishop**
   (Greek: *episkopos*) which means *overseer*. It is the Scriptural name given to the position, the person's office.

3. **Apostle** – used approximately 81 times in the New Testament.
   Prophet – used approximately 9 times in the New Testament, of New Testament prophets.
   Evangelist – used approximately 3 times in the New Testament.
   Shepherd – used approximately 17 times in the New Testament; once as a *pastor*, 16 times as *shepherd*.
   Teacher – used approximately 60 times as *master* or *teacher*.

Therefore,
   The word **elder** describes the **man**.
   The word **bishop** describes the **office**.
   The words **apostle, prophet, evangelist, shepherd** and **teacher** describe the **work**.

IN SUMMARY:

In _____ Christian Fellowship, we endeavour to recognise and receive gifted ministries in their particular ministries and in their particular office or function, without using titles. The New Testament called them by name, not by title.

Those who are of the fivefold ministries and those who are elders are recognised together as **the Eldership** and this group is responsible for the government of the local church. In this Eldership it is recognised and accepted that there is someone who is the Senior Minister by reason of the gift and grace bestowed upon him by the Lord.

By this form of Church Government, we endeavour to have Biblical "checks and balances" against becoming an "autocracy", or "bureaucracy", or the congregation becoming a "democracy", and other pitfalls arising from forms of government which have little or no accountability. These can be observed in church history. Some of these are seen in the following four types of church government:

1. **AUTOCRACY**
    - The rule of the one man, without checks and balances.

2. **BUREAUCRACY**
    - The rule of the few, and "hire and fire" system in the church.

3. **DEMOCRACY**
    - The rule of the people, mass rule, electing and controlling the oversight.

4. **HIERARCHY**
    - External control by a central organisational body.

We believe that the fifth type of church government is the one that best reflects the New Testament and provides the structure that allows the Lord Jesus His rightful place as the ruling Head of the Church.

5. **THEOCRACY**
    - The rule of Christ as Head of the Church through His appointed ministries, having proper checks and balances in the government of His Church through the Eldership, leaders and the congregation (Ephesians 5:21). The congregation does have a voice, but does not exercise rule over the oversight or the ministry.

CHECKS AND BALANCES

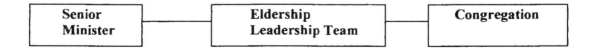

| Senior Minister | Eldership Leadership Team | Congregation |

"A THREEFOLD CORD IS NOT QUICKLY BROKEN" (Ecclesiastes 4:12).

APPLICATION FOR MEMBERSHIP

For those who desire to make_____Christian Fellowship their church home, and become a voluntary committed member, this form should be filled out and then approved by the Eldership.

PLEASE FILL IN THE FOLLOWING PARTICULARS.

NAME _____ DATE OF BIRTH _____

ADDRESS _____

POSTCODE _____ TELEPHONE _____

PARTICULARS FOR MEMBERSHIP.

1. Are you a new convert? Yes / No* Conversion Date _____

2. TRANSFER OF MEMBERSHIP. Because our desire is to follow ministerial ethics and maintain good relations with other churches, before approving you for membership, we ask you to answer the questions below.

Have you been a member of another church?   Yes / No*

If Yes, what is the name of the previous church you attended? _____

Minister's name: _____   Phone no. _____

What was the reason for leaving your previous church and coming to _____ Christian Fellowship?

_____

_____

If necessary, may we contact your previous minister for reference?   Yes / No*

FOR BOTH NEW CONVERTS AND THOSE TRANSFERRING MEMBERSHIP.

1. I have received Jesus Christ as my personal Saviour and Lord. Yes / No*

2. I have been baptised as a believer in water.   Yes / No*   Date _____

3. I have been baptised in the Holy Spirit. Yes / No*   Date _____

4. If "No" to 2 & 3, do you desire baptism in water and in the Holy Spirit? Yes / No*

5. How many sessions of "Foundational Principles of Church Membership" have you completed? _____
If you have not completed all the sessions, they will need to be finished by tape.

6. Do you believe in the doctrines of faith as have been taught in the "Foundational Principles of Church Membership"? Yes / No*

7. By God's grace, will you support the work of the Lord in this local church by tithes and offerings?

8. By God's grace, will your lifestyle be consistent with Christian conduct and doctrine?

9. Do you desire to become a voluntary committed member of _____Christian Fellowship and submit yourself to the oversight of the church, who are also committed to your care?

9. Have you read the Constitution?   Yes / No* If you have any questions, feel free to see one of the Elders.

SIGNATURE _____   DATE _____

*Circle whichever word is applicable to you.

SUPPLEMENTAL
("SAMPLE" CONSTITUTION FOR MEMBERSHIP IN A LOCAL CHURCH)

The Australian Government requires that non-profit and Religious Corporations have a Constitution, and more especially to protect the interests of those members who give funds and invest their interests in the purchase of lands and/or buildings.

APPLICATION FOR MEMBERSHIP

A natural person who applies and is approved for membership as provided in these rules is eligible to become a member of the Fellowship.

1. A person who is not a member of the Fellowship at the time of the incorporation of the Fellowship (or who was such a member at that time but has ceased to be a member) shall not be admitted unless the person meets the following qualifications:

   (a) Personal faith in the Lord Jesus Christ as their Lord and Saviour, and a desire to obey the requirements laid down in Acts 2:36-47.
   (b) Agreement with the Doctrines of Faith.
   (c) A lifestyle that is consistent with Christian conduct and doctrine.
   (d) Regular attendance at the activities of the Fellowship.
   (e) Willingness to obey the Biblical commands regarding tithes and free-will offerings for the financial support of the Fellowship. See Rule 34.
   (f) Voluntary submission to the spiritual oversight of the Fellowship.
   (g) Completion of "Foundational Principles of Church Membership".
   (h) Application for membership.
   (i) Admission as a member first recommended by the Senior Minister and then approved by the Eldership.

2. An application of a person for membership of the Fellowship:
   (a) shall be made in such form as is approved by the Senior Minister; and
   (b) shall be made to, or lodged with, any member of the Eldership.

3. As soon as practicable after its receipt, the application shall be transferred to the Senior Minister.

4. Upon an application being referred to the Senior Minister, the Senior Minister shall determine whether to recommend or to reject the application.

5. Upon an application being recommended by the Senior Minister, the Senior Minister shall call a meeting of the Eldership who shall determine whether to approve or reject the recommendation of the Senior Minister.

6. Upon an application being approved or rejected by the Eldership, the applicant shall be notified that he or she has been approved or rejected for membership of the Fellowship.

7. Individuals accepted for membership will receive the right hand of fellowship (Galatians 2:9) and receive a membership certificate at a Membership Commitment Service. The applicant's name shall be entered into the Register of Members kept for the purpose and, upon the name being so entered, the applicant becomes a member of the Fellowship.

8. A right, privilege or obligation of persons by reason of their membership of the Fellowship:
   (a) is not capable of being transferred or transmitted to another person;
   (b) terminates upon the cessation of their membership whether by death or resignation or otherwise as set out in these rules.

ENTRANCE FEE

There shall be no entrance fee or annual subscription fee, but members are expected to consistently give tithes and offerings to support to Fellowship's ministry.

REGISTER OF MEMBERSHIP

A Register of Members shall be kept and maintained, in which shall be entered the full name, address, telephone number(s), email address, and date of acceptance of the name of each member, and the Register shall be available for inspection by members at the address of the Fellowship.

RESIGNATION OR DELETION OF MEMBERS

1. A member of the Fellowship may resign from the Fellowship at any time by serving notice in writing to the Eldership. Such a resignation shall take effect immediately.

2. Upon receipt of such a notice, an entry recording the date upon which the member resigned shall be made in the Register of Members.

3. The Eldership shall review the list of members annually, and may delete any persons that, in the opinion of the Eldership, should not continue as members of the Fellowship.

4. For the purpose of membership, the criteria to be used by the Eldership may include consideration of whether the person, in the opinion of the Eldership, has, is or is likely to satisfy the following criteria:

   (a) the person seeks to maintain a proper relationship with the Lord;
   (b) attends worship on a regular basis;
   (c) participates in other activities of the Fellowship on a regular basis;
   (d) seeks to discover and exercise their spiritual gifts for the benefit of the Fellowship;
   (e) consistently gives tithes and offerings to support the Fellowship's ministries;
   (f) shares in commitment to, and the fulfilment of the philosophy and vision of the Fellowship; and
   (g) comes under the authority and protection of the appointed leadership in line with Hebrews 13:17.

5. The Eldership may delete a member from the Register of Members if such member has not, without reasonable excuse or leave of absence granted by the Senior Minister or the Eldership, attended for any consecutive period of 13 weeks, the normal and regular worship meetings of the Fellowship.

6. Any member who has been deleted from the Register of Members may apply to the Eldership for reinstatement of his or her membership.

7. The Eldership in considering any application shall by resolution determine whether or not to reinstate the membership of the applicant.

DISCIPLINE OF MEMBERS

1. Subject to these Rules, the Biblical principles set out in Matthew 18:15-20; 5:23-26 and Galatians 6:1-5; 2 John 9-11; Hebrews 10:25; Romans 6:17-18, and the moral standards set out in 1 Corinthians 5:9-13; Romans 1:18-32; 2 Thessalonians 3:6-18 and Leviticus 18; the Eldership may determine to:

   (a) expel a member from membership of the Fellowship; or
   (b) suspend a member from membership of the Fellowship for a specified period – if the Eldership is of the opinion that the member:

      (i) has refused or neglected to comply with these rules;
      (ii) failed to uphold and maintain the aforementioned moral standards; or
      (iii) has been guilty of conduct unbecoming of a member or which is prejudicial to the interests of the Fellowship.

   (The purpose of discipline is restorative and remedial. However, if a person is separated from the Fellowship, they may not be reinstated until there has been a genuine repentance of the offence and reconciliation, which will be attested to by the Senior Minister and confirmed by the Eldership.)

2. A determination of the Eldership does not take effect unless the Eldership, at a meeting held not earlier than seven (7) and not later than fourteen (14) days after the service on the member of a notice, confirms their previous determination, after giving an opportunity for the member to be expelled or suspended to be heard.

3. Where the Eldership makes a determination, the Secretary shall, as soon as practicable, cause to be served to the member a notice in writing:

   (a) setting out the determination of the Eldership and the grounds on which it is based;
   (b) stating that the member may address the Eldership at a meeting to be held not earlier than seven (7) and not later than fourteen (14) days after the service on the member of the notice;
   (c) stating the date, place and time of that meeting; and
   (d) informing the member that he or she may do one or more of the following:
      (i) attend the meeting;
      (ii) give to the Eldership before the date of that meeting a written statement seeking the revocation of that determination.

4. At a meeting of the Eldership held in accordance with Rule 5, the Eldership:
   (a) shall give to the member an opportunity to be heard;
   (b) shall give due consideration to any written statement submitted by the member; and
   (c) shall by resolution determine whether to confirm or revoke the determination of the Eldership.

5. A member aggrieved by the determination or a resolution of the Eldership shall have no right of appeal, or to request a general meeting of the members to consider such determination or resolution as the case may be.

CONCLUSION

There is no obligation on anyone to apply for membership once the "Foundational Principles of Church Membership" has been completed. It is perfectly acceptable for a person to go through the series as a means of becoming familiar with the foundational teaching of the Fellowship.

However, if after the completion of the "Foundational Principles of Church Membership" you believe that the Lord is planting you in _____ Christian Fellowship, please fill in the Membership Application form.

You will be notified of your acceptance, and you will be received into membership of the Fellowship at a special Membership Commitment Service. You will be notified of the date for this service in due time.

NOTE:

If, at any time, you are transferred to another location, travel interstate, or in the will of God, transfer to another Fellowship, we do ask that you contact or write to the Eldership for a letter of release and/or reference for your new home church. We are committed to your care and welfare while you are at _____ Christian Fellowship.

"FOUNDATIONAL PRINCIPLES OF CHURCH MEMBERSHIP"

CLASS ANSWER SHEETS

Lesson One - The New Testament Church

A.   What is the Church:
1. The Church is not:
   (a) A material building
   (b) A denomination
   (c) An extension of Judaism (or, the Jew's religion)

2. The Church is:
   (a) The Ecclesia – "The Called Out Company"
   (b) The Ecclesia – "The Assembled People of God"
   (c) The Habitation of God by the Spirit
   (d) The Body of Christ in the earth

D.
1. Added to the Lord
2. Added to the Church

E.
1. Repentance from dead works
2. Faith towards God
3. Water Baptism
4. Holy Spirit Baptism
5. Apostles' Doctrine (Teaching)
6. Fellowship
7. Breaking of Bread
8. Prayers

F.
1. Ministry to the Lord
2. Ministry to the Saints
3. Ministry to the World

Lesson Two - Repentance from Dead Works

A.
1. Repent
2. Believe

B.   Repentance is not:
1. Conviction of sin
2. Worldly sorrow
3. Reformation
4. Being religious
5. Mental faith

C.   Works

D.   Fruit

E.   1. Godly sorrow for sin
       2. Confession of sin
       3. Forsaking of sin
       4. Hatred of sin
       5. Restitution (where possible)

Lesson Three – Faith Towards God

A.   1. Believe
       2. Repentance and faith
       3. Repentance and faith
       4. Faith towards God

B.   1. That He exists
       2. Believe on His Name

C.   1. Faith is not natural faith (what we see, hear, touch, smell and touch)
       2. Faith is not mental faith (mental acceptance of God)
       3. Faith is not presumption
       4. Faith is not faith in yourself

E.   Faith comes by hearing and hearing by the Word of God

F.   1. " The measure of faith"
       2. Little faith
       3. Great faith
       4. Perfect faith

H.   1. A new identity
       2. A new nature
       3. A new power
       4. A new Lord of my life
       5. A new value system
       6. A new peace
       7. A new purpose
       8. A new destiny

Lesson Four – Water Baptism

A.   To put into or under water so as to entirely immerse or submerge

C.   Repentance and Faith
D.   1. Death
       2. Burial
       3. Resurrection

F.   Obey the Great Commission

Lesson Five – Holy Spirit Baptism

C.
1. Born of the Spirit
2. Filled with the Spirit
3. Led by the Spirit
4. Ministered by the Spirit
5. Cast out demons by the Spirit
6. Anointed with the Spirit
7. Offered up on the cross by the power of the Spirit
8. Raised from the dead by the Spirit
9. Gave commandments by the Spirit

G.
3
(a) To pray
(b) We will receive what we ask for

4.
(a) Repentance and faith
(b) Hunger
(c) Asking
(d) Expecting

Lesson Six – The Apostles' Doctrine

A. Teaching/Instruction
(a) God
(b) Christ
(c) Demons
(d) Men
(e) Apostles

1. Character
2. Attitudes/Beliefs
3. Behaviour/Lifestyle
4. Destiny

Lesson Seven – Praise and Worship

B.
1. Spirit
2. Truth

C. A believer is a priest to God who offers spiritual sacrifices

D.
1. At all times
2. Continually
3. While I have my being
4. As long as I live

D.
1. On our beds
2. In the congregation
3. World – unsaved

G.   1.   With our mouths
     2.   With our h ands – clapping/lifting/playing instruments
     3.   With our bodies – standing/bowing/kneeling/dancing

Lesson Eight – Fellowship

B.   1. Godward
         (a) The Father
         (b) The Son
         (c) The Holy Spirit

     2. Manward
         (a) One another
         (b) The saints

C.   1.   The world
     2.   Demon spirits
     3.   Unrighteousness
     4.   False religion
     5.   False doctrines
     6.   Disorderly conduct

Lesson Nine – The Lord's Table

A.   1.   The Lord's Supper
     2.   The Lord's Table
     3.   The Communion
     4.   The Eucharist

D.   2.   Christ's broken body
          The Church, the Body of Christ
     4.   The Blood of the New Covenant

G.   1.   Christ's death and resurrection – 1Cor.11:26
     2.   Christ's second coming – 1Cor.11:26
     3.   Believers are brothers and sisters in God's family –
          1Cor.10:16-17. We are one body.

H.   1.   Health and healing
          Life, hope and resurrection
     2.   Guilty of the body and blood of our Lord
          Judgment to oneself
          Weakness, sickness and premature death

Lesson Ten – Christian Stewardship

B.   1.   Our life
     2.   Our time
     3.   Our talents and abilities

           4. Our possessions

           5. Our finances

D   1. Wasting his master's possessions

          2. Call him to account

          3. Yes

          4. Shrewdness

          5. That we are accountable, that we must be faithful in using that which is not our own

Lesson Eleven – Church Membership

Lesson Twelve – Local Church Government

C.   1. Elders in every church

          2. Elders in Jerusalem

          3. Elders at Jerusalem

          4. Elders of Ephesus

          5. Elders of Jerusalem

          6. Let the elders that rule

          7. Call for the elders

          8. The elders among you

          9. Ordain elders in every city

          10. Obey them that have the rule

About the Author

Born in Melbourne, Australia in 1927 and saved at the age of 14, Kevin Conner served the Lord in the Salvation Army until the age of 21. At this time he entered pastoral ministry for several years. After that, he was involved in teaching ministry in Australia, New Zealand and for many years at Bible Temple in Portland, Oregon. After serving as Senior Minister of Waverley Christian Fellowship for eight years (1987-1994), he continued to serve the church locally as well as ministering at various conferences and the continued writing of textbooks.

Kevin is recognised internationally as a teaching-apostle after his many years in both church and Bible College ministry. His textbooks have been used by ministers and students throughout the world. He has been in great demand as a teacher and has travelled extensively. Kevin passed away peacefully in Melbourne, Australia in February 2019 at the age of 92.

Visit Kevin's web site at <u>www.kevinconner.org</u> for more details about his life and ministry, as well as information about his 75+ books, his video courses, and his audio teaching podcast.

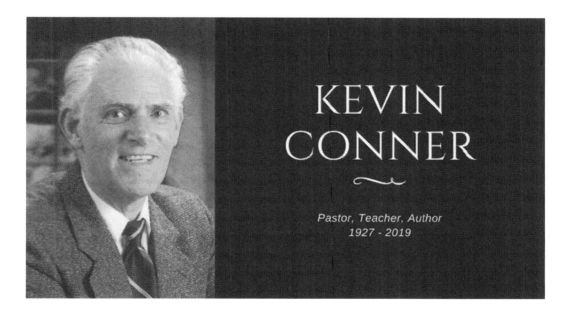

KEVIN CONNER

Pastor, Teacher, Author
1927 - 2019

Kevin's Autobiography

Kevin Conner is known by many people around the world as a theologian, Bible teacher, and best-selling author of over 75 biblical textbooks. Although thousands of people have been impacted by his ministry and his writings, only a few people know his personal story. Kevin took the time to detail his own life journey, including lessons gleaned along the way, in his auto-biography "This is My Story" back in 2007. It is now available in the following formats:

- PDF download - visit www.kevinconner.org/shop
- International paperback or eBook from Amazon.
- Australian paperback from WORD books (www.word.com.au).

Kevin was an orphan who never met his dad or mum. He grew up in boy's homes before coming to faith in Jesus Christ in the Salvation Army in his teenage years. From there, his life took many turns as he continued to pursue his faith in God and his understanding of the Scriptures and church life. Follow his journey and gain wisdom for your own life and ministry as you read his intriguing life-story.

Other Books by Kevin Conner

Acts, A Commentary
An Evaluation of Joseph Prince's Book 'Destined to Reign'
Are Women Elders Biblical?
Biblical Principles of Leadership
The Christian Millennium
1 & 2 Chronicles, a Commentary
1 Corinthians, a Commentary
The Church in the New Testament
The Church of the Firstborn and the Birthright
1 & 2 Chronicles, A Commentary
Colossians and Philemon, A Commentary
The Covenants (with Ken Malmin)
Daily Devotions (or Ministrations)
Daniel, An Exposition
The Day After the Sabbath
The Death-Resurrection Route
Deuteronomy, A Commentary
Esther, A Commentary
Exodus, A Commentary
Ezekiel, A Commentary
The Feasts of Israel
First Principles of the Doctrine of Christ
Foundations of Christian Doctrine
Foundations of Christian Doctrine (Self Study Guide)
Foundational Principles of Church Membership
Foundation Principles of the Doctrine of Christ
Frequently Asked Questions
Galatians, A Commentary
Genesis, A Commentary
Headship, Covering and Hats
Hebrews, A Commentary
The House of God
Interpreting the Book of Revelation
Interpreting the Scriptures (with Ken Malmin)
Interpreting the Scriptures (Self Study Guide)
Interpreting the Symbols and Types
Isaiah, A Commentary
James, A Commentary
Jeremiah and Lamentations, A Commentary
Joshua, A Commentary
Jude, A Commentary
Judges, A Commentary
Keep Yourself Pure

The Kingdom Cult of Self
Kings of the Kingdom - Character Studies on Israel's Kings
Law and Grace
Leviticus, A Commentary
The Lord Jesus Christ our Melchizedek Priest
Maintaining the Presence
Marriage, Divorce and Remarriage
Messages from Matthew
Methods and Principles of Bible Research
Ministries in the Cluster
The Ministry of Women
The Minor Prophets, A Commentary Mystery
Mystery Parables of the Kingdom
The Name of God
New Covenant Realities
New Testament Survey (with Ken Malmin)
Numbers, A Commentary
Old Testament Survey (with Ken Malmin)
Only for Catholics
Passion Week Chart
Philippians, A Commentary
Psalms, A Commentary
The Relevance of the Old Testament to a New Testament Church Restoration Theology
Restoration Theology
Revelation, A Commentary
Romans, A Commentary
The Royal Seed
Ruth, A Commentary
1 & 2 Samuel, A Commentary
Sermon Outlines (3 volumes)
The Seventy Weeks Prophecy
Studies in the Royal Priesthood
The Sword and Consequences
The Tabernacle of David
The Tabernacle of Moses
The Temple of Solomon
Table Talks
Tale of Three Trees
1 & 2 Thessalonians, A Commentary
This is My Story (Kevin Conner's autobiography)
This We Believe
Three Days and Three Nights (with Chart)
Tithes and Offerings
Today's Prophets
To Drink or Not to Drink

To Smoke or Not to Smoke
Two Kings and a Prince
Understanding the New Birth and the Baptism of the Holy Spirit
Vision of an Antioch Church
Water Baptism Thesis
What About Israel?

Visit www.kevinconner.org for more information.
Visit www.amazon.com/author/kevinjconner for a list of other books by Kevin Conner.

Video Training Seminars

Kevin Conner's popular "Key of Knowledge" Seminar is now available as an online teaching course. Part 1 covers 'Methods and Principles of Bible Research' and includes over 6 hours of video teaching, the required textbooks, extra hand out notes, and a self-guided online study program. The first lesson, 'Challenge to Study' is FREE.

The second part of Kevin Conner's "Key of Knowledge" Seminar is about 'Interpreting the Bible' and includes over 7 hours of video teaching, two downloadable textbooks, extra hand out notes, and a self-guided online study program. These two courses can be taken as stand-alone courses, in succession, or simultaneously.

Also available at www.kevinconner.org/courses is Kevin's extensive teaching on his best-selling book The Foundation of Christian Doctrine, which includes 67 videos which can be purchased in 4 parts.

Visit the courses page at www.kevinconner.org for all the details.

Kevin Conner's Audio Teaching

Dozens of Kevin Conner's messages are available on his FREE teaching podcast - 'Kevin Conner Teaches'. This podcast is accessible from Apple Podcasts, Google Podcasts, or Spotify Podcasts (if you are a subscriber), as well as at www.kevinconner.podbean.com (including on the Podbean mobile App).

New messages are published weekly, selected from messages Kevin has given over the years at various churches, conferences, and training seminars. Be sure to subscribe so you are notified of recent releases.

Visit https://www.kevinconner.org/audios-by-kevin/ for a full list of podcast titles and series.

PDF Versions of Kevin Conner's Books

All of Kevin Conner's books are now available to purchase in quality PDF format. This digital format is in addition to the Kindle eBooks and paperback/hardback versions currently available. A PDF is a 'portable document format' used on all computers for reading documents. Books in this format can be read on a computer, laptop, or handheld device and/or printed out for your personal use (even stored in your own binding of choice). Many PDF readers also allow you to 'mark-up' and add your own notes to the document. PDFs of Kevin's books are for your personal use and are not for copying or redistribution.

You can purchase PDF books at www.kevinconner.org/shop. Upon payment, a download link will be sent to you via email along with your receipt.

Resources by Mark Conner

Kevin Conner's son, Mark Conner, worked closely with him in the church ministry for many years (as music director and youth pastor), before succeeding him in 1995 as the Senior Minister of what was then Waverley Christian Fellowship (now CityLife Church) Mark transitioned out of that role in early 2017 and since that time has been giving himself to speaking, training, coaching, and writing.

Here is a list of Mark's books which may be of interest to you:

* *Transforming Your Church - Seven Strategic Shifts*
* *Money Talks: Practical Wisdom for Becoming Financially Free*
* *The Spiritual Journey: Understanding the Stages of Faith*
* *How to Avoid Burnout: Five Habits of Healthy Living*
* *Prison Break: Finding Personal Freedom*
* *Pass the Baton: Successful Leadership Transition*
* *Successful Christian Ministry*

These can be purchased from:
* Amazon.com/author/markconner in paperback **and eBook** format.
* WORD books in Australia (www.word.com.au)
* www.kevinconner.org/books-by-mark-conner/ in **PDF** format.

Mark also has an active BLOG and teaching podcast. Visit www.markconner.com.au for more information.